A Continent Called Palestine

One woman's story

Najwa Kawar Farah

TRIANGLE

First published in Great Britain in 1996
Triangle
SPCK
Holy Trinity Church
Marylebone Road
London NW1 4DU

British Library Cataloguing-in-Publication Data
A catalogue record of this book is available from
the British Library

ISBN 0-281-04912-2

Typeset by Dorwyn Ltd, Rowlands Castle, Hants
Printed in Great Britain by BPC Paperbacks Ltd.

Contents

Foreword

In January 1996 my wife Gill and I travelled down with Najwa Farah and her husband Rafiq from Nazareth through the Jordan valley and then up past Jericho to Jerusalem. Though I had met Najwa before, it had been before I had ever set foot in Palestine. She had given me some of her books to read and I had been fascinated by the stories – by their beauty and their pain. But I hadn't seen her for many years and it was only as she started to talk as we left Nazareth and to describe her childhood memories as she pointed to the various hills around, that I recognized her.

It was a most amusing journey. Rafiq was sitting at the front of the coach and we called on him to give a running commentary, though Najwa had to keep correcting him – after all he had come from Shef'amr, not Nazareth itself! We were a sort of Episcopal road show of Bishops and visitors from all around the world that had come to Jerusalem for the consecration of the new Anglican Bishop, Riah Abu El-Assal, himself from Nazareth. From Jerusalem, we'd headed to Bethlehem for the Greek Orthodox Christmas Eve, where the two Anglican Bishops, Bishop Samir Kafity and Bishop Riah, had led President Yasser Arafat around the Church of the Nativity and then on Sunday we'd gone up to Nazareth to see the new Bishop welcomed by his own community. Now exhausted and joyful, we headed home, laughing and swapping stories. It was an optimistic time, before the suicide bombers in Jerusalem and the Israeli bombardment of Lebanon that threw the peace process into such disarray.

As I read *A Continent Called Palestine* so many friends appeared on the pages and I was captivated by the stories, but my emotions went on a roller coaster ride, for this is the rarely-told story of a land taken, a people oppressed and the everyday pain with which the people of Palestine have to live. Najwa's experience of invasion and brutal occupation is second to none as she was in Nazareth when Israeli forces came in '48. She was in the West Bank when they came in '67 and in Beirut in '82, during that invasion with its huge loss of life.

But Najwa's story comes from another angle. It is the story of the Palestinian people with their wonderful heritage trying to survive amidst all the pain and conflict. Najwa paints a picture of a dignified culture and community, where Christian and Muslim live together. It's the story of a people whose love for the land was so great that one Palestinian refugee who has just half an hour to leave his home, takes nothing but instead walks into his orchard to say goodbye to his trees.

You can read the history of this situation, the theology and the politics – and you should – but here you meet the human family and you see the world through different eyes – through the eyes of people who emerged from the colonialism of the Ottoman empire only to discover that they still mean nothing to the powerful of the world. Sometimes the pain is too great – you feel your heart bursting – this is the story that still goes on, of homes blown up, of a people trampled on and treated as nothing.

Najwa is a poet and story-teller and with her words paints pictures that tell of a beautiful life in a beautiful land and then what occupation really means. For a Christian it is almost too painful to bear as fundamentalist believers arrive and tell her that the driving out of the Palestinians was an act of God. 'Was it God's will to disinherit them, some in just one night or one hour, turning them into refugees in caves and camps, homeless, lost, condemned and dispossessed . . . was this really the will of God? That a whole people should be thrown out, subjected to such suffering? How could Christians believe that God, Creator of heaven and earth, Father of Jesus Christ who became incarnate for us human beings and for our salvation, would thus treat the very creation he came to redeem? To throw out a people which he created, to bring in others whom he favoured above all?' (pages 54–5).

And so a theology of liberation emerges in these pages, a theology of a God who is not a tribal God, who is not a primitive God but is inclusive as opposed to exclusive. A gospel of hope shines through to combat the gospel of bondage. Battered and bruised Palestine still has so much to teach us about the nature of God, about the value of human beings, and as I read Najwa's moving story I found myself praying for the wonderful Palestinian community that has given me so much hospitality and taught me so much. A year or so back I tried in a song to express some of the tentative hope that the peace process was bringing.

Oh Palestine

Uncertain footsteps on a pathway to peace
Emerging through the pain of time
Are there green shoots on the old olive tree
Is this your hour, oh Palestine?

Oh Palestine, oh Palestine
Slowly emerging – it's your turn to shine
Is this your moment – is this your time?
Is this your hour, oh Palestine?

I've seen your children behind the wire
Hidden from view from the eyes of the world
I've seen your homes taken, destroyed
Now is this your time, oh Palestine?

Oh Palestine, oh Palestine
Slowly emerging – it's your turn to shine
Is this your moment – is this your time?
Is this your hour, oh Palestine?

. . . I pray that it is.

Garth Hewitt

Acknowledgements

My sincere thanks go to Naomi Starkey. Without her patience and encouragement this book would not have seen the light of day. Also, I would like to thank my husband for reading my script and making his comments.

I would also like to explain that I elaborated on the Christian feasts in Nazareth because they give a fascinating insight into the home town of Jesus.

1
Our
Palestinian Heritage

Nazareth: the Town of Mary

Any person's life is complex. Their life is not only what happens to them, but also what is going on within. St Teresa of Avila speaks of the castle of the soul and its many chambers: the inner life which we all have. In my case, though, my inner life seemed to take over. It was as if there were two lives – this inner one and then me struggling to cope with the outside world. A world of dreams suited me better, but I had to pull myself together and try to cope. I am still trying.

My maiden name was Najwa 'Aref Kawar. Najwa means 'meditation'. It was not a common name at the time and I do not know of anybody of my age who has this name, although now it is quite common. While not a specially religious man, my father always told me that on the day I was born, he wondered at this miracle of creation, his firstborn child, and thought about God. Then he said to himself, 'What am I doing? I am meditating! I must call her Najwa!' My sister's name was Nuha, meaning 'reasoning' and my brother's name, 'Irfan, means 'mystical enlightenment'. Most Arabic names are chosen for their meaning – 'Aadil (just), Jameel (beautiful), Amin (faithful), even Jihad (struggle).

My father and mother, 'Aref and Adma, were Palestinians who came from Nazareth, where I was born in the time of the British Mandate. Like all Arab Christian families, we could trace our origins back to the ancient church of the apostles, although the popular misconception in the West is that there are no Arab Christians apart from those who were converted to Christianity through the missionaries who mostly came to the Middle East in the nineteenth century. Both my parents grew up under the Turkish Government of the Ottoman Empire. Like all their generation, they spoke bitterly of this totalitarian rule and their aspirations for liberation, and the struggle of the whole Arab world to free itself from the shackles of what was known as 'the sick man of Europe'.

My father was Greek Orthodox and came from a very large family – my grandfather had had ten sons and four daughters. After the death of his wife he married again and had his fifth daughter from the second marriage. He inherited much wealth from his father Tạnous Kawar (my great-grandfather), the first mayor of Nazareth, who owned a lot of land and built public baths, a soap factory, stable, a khan and a sesameh press as well as a number of houses.

I remember my grandfather as a very old, frail man, blue-eyed and fair, bedridden because of a stroke. Whenever there was a beautiful rose blooming in our garden, my father would cut it and tell me to give it to my grandfather. I would go to the big house and enter his room and my step-grandmother would tell him who I was, which was necessary because he had about forty grandchildren. He would take the rose, I would kiss his hand and he would open a velvet bag and give me a coin, asking if everything was going well with me.

My father had trained as a dentist in Damascus and his clinic was on the first floor of our house. He was a man with a great sense of humour, a sharp wit, but he was also quick-tempered and could fly into a rage, although he cooled down again in no time at all. He loved reading, especially poetry, and when in later years he grew old and sick, he would keep a little note-book and write down the verses he liked best, especially those by Al Muttanabi. This tenth-century poet, considered to be unequalled among Arab poets, was part of the court of Sayf-edawlah, prince of Aleppo, in the north of Syria, which is one of the most ancient cities in the world. Although many of his friends were prominent people, my father liked simple things and hated to be in debt. While he was not an ascetic man, he would call us and make us stand before him to repeat the following: 'I don't have – I don't need.'

My mother belonged to the Arab Anglican church. After the death of her father, when she was eight, she was sent with her other sisters to an orphanage, also known as the Prussian School because of the origins of its founders. It was and still is a land-mark on one of the hills of Nazareth, a huge building with 108 steps leading up to it. Generations of little girls from Nazareth were brought up in this school. The regime was harsh when it was first founded by the Society for Female Education in the East, but all the same it was a very good school that gave its pupils a training in housekeeping and an elementary education, as well as lots of Bible study and attendance at church twice every Sunday for matins and evensong.

My aunts and my mother all became teachers and worked very hard during the First World War to save money and pay their brothers' education fees, teaching all day and then sitting up late into the night, sewing. Both my uncles were sent to Bishop Gobat School in Jerusalem, built by the second Anglican Bishop in Jerusalem, Samuel Gobat (1847–1879). It took them three days to get to the city, riding on horseback. My elder uncle, Elias, was later ordained as an Anglican vicar, while the younger, Aziz, studied medicine at the Syrian Protestant College in Beirut (founded in 1863 and later known as The American University of Beirut).

A Community in Exile

One of the episodes which my mother told me hundreds of times and which I was always excited to hear, was about my uncle Elias who, during the First World War, was in Nablus, the largest city in the West Bank, about sixty kilometres north of Jerusalem. The Turkish military authorities suspected the Protestant Church of being pro-British because it was affiliated to the Church of England, and thought the people might be plotting to overthrow the government.

One day, in the spring of 1918, they descended on my uncle's house and searched every Bible and hymnbook. On the following Sunday the Turkish commander with his soldiers appeared in the front seats of the church to listen to my uncle's sermon. Then they arrested him along with other local dignitaries, imprisoned them and sentenced them to death by hanging. At the last minute, the sentence was changed to banishing the whole community – eighty of them – to the city of Urpha, near the Euphrates river in southern Turkey. With tears in her eyes, my mother told of how my grandmother knelt and thanked God for sparing her son's life. She also remembered how they had to sell most of their furniture and take into exile only the clothes, bedding and cooking pots that they could carry.

A week-long train journey took them to Aleppo, during which

time they were sleeping on their belongings and were forbidden to leave the train. Travelling on, they came to the end of the railway line and had to continue their journey to Urpha on foot, young and old alike. Ordered at first to make their homes in the ruins of the houses of the Armenians, who had been victims of the terrible Turkish massacres, they refused and were eventually allowed to rent places in the city. As the course of the war changed and the exiles heard of Palestinian cities falling to the British, they applied for leave to return home to Nablus in Palestine, which was finally granted. My mother told of paying large sums of money to be allowed on the last train leaving Aleppo, of seeing the armies of the Germans and their Turkish allies in scattered retreat, and of walking for hours through countryside littered with the dead and decaying bodies of soldiers.

My father would sometimes tell another story from the First World War, when Nazareth was the headquarters of the Germans. There were already British soldiers infiltrating Nazareth and one evening, as my father was going down one of the alleys in the city, he saw a young British soldier huddling in the shadows, frightened, wounded and in great pain. My father picked him up and carried him into hiding, looked after him, and saw him out of danger. The soldier, whose first name was Horace, never forgot this good turn and carried on writing to my father. He sent photographs of himself and his family and I still remember the fine faces, the women's beautiful dresses and hats with feathers in them. Even during the Second World War, this man sent my father a letter, wanting to know that he was well and in no danger because of the war.

At this time, the future of my homeland was being decided by foreign powers. On 16 May 1916 the secret Sykes-Picot agreement was signed, to divide Greater Syria (the four provinces of the conquered Ottoman Empire) between Britain and France. On 2 November 1917, the British Government signed the Balfour Declaration, pledging support for establishing a Jewish national homeland in Palestine. On 9 December 1917, allied forces under General Allenby entered Jerusalem and by September 1918 the whole of Palestine was occupied. The Paris Peace Conference on 1919 decided that the conquered Arab provinces would not be restored to Ottoman rule and on 25 April 1920, the Supreme Council of the San Remo Peace Conference assigned the mandate for governing Palestine to Britain – without the consent of the Palestinians.

2
Childhood in Nazareth

My home town of Nazareth lies in southern Galilee, eighteen miles east of Haifa and sixteen miles south-west of Tiberias. The first impression you had of it when approaching by road was of white convents and dark green cypress trees. When I was a child, we often spent Sunday afternoons walking in the surrounding hills, especially in spring when we picked flowers – anemones and cyclamen. Thyme and many other herbs scented the air. From the hills you could see the plain of Merj ibn Amir (the Arabic name for the Valley of Jezreel or the Plain of Esdraelon, mentioned in the Old Testament) and my father would point out the different villages in it. Further away, you could see Mount Tabor and on a clear day you could see as far as Mount Carmel. The far-off hills had soft hues of blue and violet. On one evening the full moon was so near between the rolling hills that it seemed to be beckoning me. I felt like running towards a different world – a world of adventure.

On other Sundays my father would take us to the woods or to picnic spots. One which lay nearby was the Austrian Hospice, a convent in the midst of a small wood and a cemetery for the Germans who fell in the First World War. If the abbot knew that my father had come with his family, he would invite us into the Mess room, give us wine and insist on taking us on a guided tour, a thing I dreaded because it always ended in the cemetery. By then it was evening, with the last rays of the sun stealing their way through the cypress trees. Walking between the lines of graves and the crosses, I felt afraid and terribly sad for the young soldiers who were forever strangers in another people's country. I clung to my mother's side, pale-faced and afraid to look back. Years later, one of the first poems I wrote was called 'Tears in the Strangers' Graveyard'.

The townspeople of Nazareth refer to any location according to its characteristic religion – the Muslim quarter, the Greek Orthodox quarter, the Latin quarter. In each of these there were smaller alleys which branched off, named after the prominent family living in that area. There were *suks* (markets) for each sort of merchandise or craft – the copper- and knife-makers, the vegetable market, the spice, the tinkers, the dyers, the *graineh* (threshing floor), rented from the local council, where corn and wheat were sold. The Nazareth which I knew also had many orchards and gardens and was famed for its apricots.

The houses of the Kawar family were adjacent to each other and formed one big complex in the centre of the town, known as the Kawars' quarter, with vaulted, cobble-stoned alleys. To reach the homes of the uncles and cousins, you sometimes did not even need to go through the alleys because there were always gates and stairs to reach one another's houses. The main house had once been beautiful, but when I knew it, it had started to fall into disrepair. It had big windows with coloured glass and a ceiling painted with garlands of flowers. The big reception room had a marble floor, painted walls, wine-coloured curtains with gold edges. I remember a tall, gilded mirror.

Living in Nazareth exposed me to a sort of ecumenism that made me accept, respect and love all Christian communities, for the hills of Nazareth and the town itself were full of all kinds of Christian communities. Approximately one-third of the people were Greek Orthodox, one-third Muslim, and one-third were what we called Western Christian communities, comprising Protestant, Greek Catholic, and Latin (Roman Catholic). The Greek Catholics were Orthodox who came under the Roman Pope in the seventeenth century but still kept their Orthodox liturgy. Families congregated near each other, but as the town expanded, they would move to wherever suited them. My mother, like most of the people of Nazareth, could discern the different rhythm and toll of each church bell as they rang on Sunday mornings. 'Those are the bells of the Greek Orthodox church. That is the bell of the Greek Catholics. That great bell is the Ave Maria.' The Ave Maria, in its beautiful belfry, was our Big Ben. Women would time their work by it, Muslim and Christian alike. It was the bell of Mary, their townswoman, for whom they cherished great love.

Nazareth people also never forgot that Jesus was their fellow countryman. Although they were proud of the fact, they were no more holy or more devout than any other people. Sometimes I used to feel that they had not changed since the times of Jesus and were still provincial unbelievers who could say about any remarkable person 'Who is he? Isn't he just the son of so-and-so?'

I went through primary school classes quickly, younger than the average age because Aunt Julia (confusingly, I had two and this Julia came from my mother's family) was the kindergarten teacher in Nazareth and she suggested to my mother that I attend her school. On my way there every day, I passed the Russian compound, known to the townspeople as *Maskoubiah* (derived from the word 'Muscovite'). Originally it was a Russian school and its proper name was the Russian Teachers' Training Seminary, founded by the Imperial Orthodox Society in Jerusalem in 1886. The Society's aim was to 'preserve the Orthodox Church in the Holy Land' and to 'darn or patch its beautiful garment rent by the societies mentioned above', referring to the Western Christian missions who were hurrying to establish their presence as the Ottoman Empire, the sick man of Europe, was on its death-bed.

This distinguished seminary under the dedicated headmaster Iskandar Kuzma (which closed down in 1914) produced many remarkable teachers among its graduates, as well as writers, journalists, poets and novelists. Among the most notable were Khalil Baidas, the first novelist in Palestine, owner of the first Arabic magazine and translator of Russian literature, and Michael Nuimeh (Lebanese) who after studying in Russia emigrated to America and was the closest friend and biographer of the illustrious Gibran Khalil Gibran (author of *The Prophet*).

Another landmark on my journey to school was the Greek Orthodox church of the Annunciation, also called the Church of the Angel Gabriel. There were two churches in Nazareth with the name of Annunciation and each congregation claimed theirs was the genuine one. The other church belonged to the Latins, built over the cave which was believed to be the site of Mary and Joseph's house. Years later, the old church was pulled down and a beautiful new basilica built and dedicated by Pope Paul VI during his visit to the Holy Land in 1964.

One of the most loved institutions in Nazareth was the Syrian Orphanage for boys, known as the Schneller School. It stood outside the town to the west and was founded by Johan Ludwig Schneller, a Prussian missionary who came to Jerusalem in 1854 at the invitation of Bishop Samuel Gobat. After the massacre of Christians by the Druze in Lebanon and Syria in 1860, he was much moved by the suffering of the orphaned children and dedicated the rest of his life to helping them, by building his vocational schools.

The schools supplied Palestine with highly skilled workers, craftsmen and teachers in many trades, teaching the boys to have pride in their work and to strive to perfect it. German was taught as a second language and they also studied musical instruments such as the flute, as well as physical training and religious education. The schools were run by Lutherans, but they never stressed their religious denomination. The boys would all come in pairs to the Anglican Church on Sunday mornings.

Although I personally had little to do with the orphanage, I was fascinated by the wooded grounds and by the training of the boys. The minute you entered the place, you sensed the healthy, though austere, atmosphere which prevailed. Nazareth people were allowed to picnic in the grounds and we used to be invited to Graduation Day when the pupils gave sports displays and musical performances. The boys also worked in the fields and harvested their own corn, and their home-made bread was famous.

After finishing primary school, every student had to choose between carpentry, working in the smithy, typing, tailoring, shoemaking, bookbinding or agriculture. For the blind boys there was basketry and canework. I must have been impressed by the spirit of this institution because I later wrote a story called 'The Orphan Artist' which won first prize from the Arabic section of the Dutch Hilversum Broadcasting Station. When Israel occupied Nazareth, it closed the school as enemy property, because it was a German institution, but there are still Schneller schools in Lebanon and Jordan, with the majority of boys in the Amman schools now coming from the Palestinian refugee camps under the voluntary headship of Sami Habiby.

Yet another landmark in Nazareth was the Edinburgh Medical Mission Society Hospital, referred to as the EMMS Hospital. The founder was Dr Varten, an Armenian, who in 1861 came from Beirut to Nazareth to work in Galilee. He started a hospital with six beds and the EMMS adopted the project in 1866. He worked tirelessly for nearly half a century – the hospital was the only one between Beirut and Jerusalem. The hospital stood on the western hills, surrounded by flower beds and beautiful groves of pine trees. It was like the biblical light on a hill, not only because of its excellent professional service, but also for its unceasing Christian witness, and its friendliness and love for the people of Nazareth and the villages round about, treating the many poor people free of charge. The whole staff, doctors and nurses, were united in their witness, sharing a desire to identify with the people of Nazareth. The tradition is still carried on.

On the main road leading to Tiberias lay Mary's Well or The Virgin's Well, built in 1862 on the site where tradition had it that Mary went to fetch water. The apocryphal story was that the angel Gabriel first appeared to her as she was on her way to the well. Terrified, she left her jar and rushed back to the house where the angel delivered his message to her. Parts of the church dated back to AD750 and on the northern side of the church there were steps leading to a vaulted room, dating from the time of the Crusaders, where you could still draw water. For us primary schoolgirls, it was always moving to go down the dark stairs where coloured oil lamps shed faint light on the well, and drink from the holy water, kneel before the altar and cross ourselves. Afterwards, we would usually leave the church to sit in the grounds and chat, but this interlude was not at all like visiting each other's houses. It was special, filling us with joy and a sense of belonging.

On Sundays I went to the Arab Anglican church with my mother, although I went to the flourishing local Baptist church for Sunday School, the boys sitting on one side and the girls on the other. We would sing hymns and, as I grew older, I would be chosen to write the week's golden text in Arabic on the blackboard. Although I was attending the Government Girls' School, my mother was not satisfied with what I was learning and set out to supplement it. I read my schoolbooks before the rest of the class had studied them, which made school boring for me, but at home my mother taught me English which was only learnt in the higher classes. She read me stories and when she went to Jerusalem, she would bring back books like *Britain and Her Neighbours* and three volumes of *New Age*. I loved those books and was dazzled by the pictures. She also brought me a beautiful book of fairy tales by Hans Christian Andersen and by the Grimm brothers. Such books furnished my world of dreams. I started writing at an early age, my imagination seeking to escape from the here and now. What I loved most was nature – trees, horizons, forests, flowers, and the sky, especially the moon and the stars.

My mother put my sister Nuha and my brother 'Irfan through the same learning process. Her motto was 'Make use of time', even when she was washing up the dishes. I would stand by to dry them and had to spell difficult English words like 'though' and 'colonel', 'chief' and 'thief' – 'i' before 'e'. Even when we were going for a walk, she would ask me the word for a female buck or a male duck and so on. Sometimes my father would say, 'Leave her to play' but I played very little. My favourite toys were wooden blocks in different shapes for building a house. My houses had an arch for a gate, green trees and windows. I spent a lot of time building and dreaming. Dolls were another fascination.

Being the eldest, I was expected to look after my sister and brother, although there were not many years between us all. When I was still very young, my parents would go visiting nearby and we would be left alone. One day I got very frightened, after reading one of the Sinbad stories from the Arabian Nights, at the thought of being in the Valley of the Skulls. In the Arabic book there was a picture of a heap of skulls and a genie roasting bodies on skewers, tiny in proportion to the laughing genie. I also grew afraid of going down to my father's dental clinic in the evening, because of a skull on top of a glass-fronted cupboard. After that, my parents would ask my stepgrandmother or Um Saleemeh (the woman who helped my mother with housework) to come and stay with us.

3
Nazareth: Our Christian Year

The changes of the seasons were always exciting, like a ritual in our lives as a family and as a community. When winter came, it gave us such joy to come back from school to a cosy home, where the rugs were laid out and the brass brazier was shining after being polished with Brasso. In the evening, my mother would boil carrots and roast chestnuts on the brazier while we sat on floor mattresses and cushions or on low wicker chairs. We would also have plates of dried figs, raisins and walnuts.

Our main meal was at lunch-time, so at supper we roasted special white cheese and had strained yoghurt with olive oil. Deliciously scented oranges would be newly arrived at the market, some sweet and with green peel, and all very cheap.

Spring was gorgeous but short. Time to go to the hills to pick flowers, thyme and other spring leaves and herbs. When summer came, the household rugs were thoroughly cleaned and then stored away. My sister and I would get out our summer dresses. Summer also meant melons and grapes, and going on holiday.

Christmas

As a child I did not like autumn, a melancholy season, but then I could begin to look forward to Christmas. In Nazareth, Christmas was more low-key than Easter which was and still is called the Great Feast. There were Christmas trees in public buildings and in some (mainly Protestant) churches and church schools. Catholic churches put more emphasis on the crib and the stable-cave.

I should mention that the Western communities in Nazareth followed the well-known Julian calendar, while the Eastern churches followed their own calendar, so that Western Christmas was on 25 December, while the Orthodox

Christmas was on 6 January. Sometimes there might be a whole forty days between the Orthodox and Western Easters.

My mother was among the first in Nazareth to introduce the Christmas tree into the home. She would bring beautiful little decorations from Jerusalem – tiny cream-coloured houses with red roofs, red and blue tinsel balls, birds swinging from silvery wreaths, Santa Claus, candleholders, angels with fluffy wings, and a gold star to put on the top. I kept some of these decorations and my own children enjoyed them when they were little.

Epiphany fell on 6 January, the Greek Orthodox Christmas. Special sweets were prepared with very thin pastry, some of it filled with nuts, cinnamon and sugar, and some fried and dipped in syrup. On 15 January, it was my brother 'Irfan's birthday. All our extended family would come for a big tea, and my father engaged the best sweetmaker to come to the house and prepare two huge trays of *kenafeh* (shredded rolls of wheat with syrup, cheese or walnuts). My mother played the organ and we all sang hymns, followed by games. After my brother's birthday, my mother would take down the Christmas tree and the Christmas decorations were put away for another year *inshallah* (God willing).

One year, while the sweets were being prepared at the party, I was jumping stairs on the first floor, starting with three, then four, five. I was ambitious and it was at about six stairs that I landed awkwardly, fell and broke my leg. Disaster! Although the birthday party went on, and the sweets and the birthday tea were served, I ended up in bed. I could hear my mother playing the organ and my family singing. The doctor put my leg in a plaster cast and for forty days I lay in bed, unable to move. My mother brought me books and I was even able to keep up with my school lessons.

Fridays and Sundays were weekly holidays for schools and government offices. Fridays were for keeping the Muslim day of prayer, Sunday for the Christians. During Lent, we went to Friday services, and during the month of Ramadan, we had half-days at school as the majority of our classmates were fasting. When evening came, a special cannon would fire once to signal the end of fasting. Many Christians would be invited to spend the evening with their Muslim friends.

Spring-cleaning was part of the yearly routine and housewives were very particular about it. It was a demanding job in which all the females in the family took part. Home help would be hired if necessary, or if people could afford it, because spring-cleaning meant stripping everything. The earthenware containers in the storeroom where the provisions were kept would be cleaned. Walls were whitewashed, doors and windows were painted.

One of the most tiring jobs was washing the mattresses which were stuffed with wool or cotton. It was a mark of prosperity to have wool-stuffed mattresses and my mother used to boast that ours were stuffed from fleece presented to my father as a wedding present by a friend who was a tribal sheikh. To Nazareth women not all wool was the same. If your mattress was stuffed with bits and pieces of wool, it was second-grade. The wool would be taken out of the covers and spread in the sun on a patio. This was important to take away the winter dampness. A long branch from the pomegranate tree would be used to beat the pressed wool and make it fluffy again. Bed quilts were always made of cotton and covered in beautiful satin-like material in blue or pink, decorated with traditional Palestinian patterns.

For cookery, it was the age of the Primus stove (and later the oil stove). On washing days, the housewife would help the washerwoman, either by rinsing the washing or hanging it out, so there was little time to cook an elaborate meal. The popular meal for that day was *mujaddarah* (lentil soup), made of crushed wheat, lentils, fried onion and olive oil, with yoghurt or tomato and spring onion salad served as a side dish.

Easter

As far as Christians were concerned, the greatest event in the life of the town was Easter. For the youngsters, it was anticipated in the way that youngsters in northern Europe look forward to Christmas. Lent was taken seriously. No meat, no fat. Instead we had tasty dishes cooked from the different herbs and leaves picked from the hills of Nazareth – *khubeizeh*, triangular spinach pastries cooked with olive oil, aubergines, stuffed vine leaves with *burgul* (crushed wheat or rice, chopped tomato, parsley and chickpeas). There was our national poor man's dish of *houmous* (chickpeas), *baba ghanoush* (aubergine salad) and *tabouleh* (crushed wheat salad). Dandelions were another tasty dish.

Each Friday afternoon in Lent there was a service of 'Songs of Praise to the Virgin Mary', while the Saturday before Palm Sunday was called in Nazareth 'Lazarus Saturday'. The preparations for this day involved dyeing boiled eggs, usually with onion skins or the flowers of the wild daisy which grew profusely on the hills of Nazareth. Young boys (six- to twelve-year olds) would be busy gluing paper into long strips to make a scroll of about a metre in length with a piece of wood attached to either end. This scroll would be painted with pictures depicting the gospel story. Very, very early on the Saturday, from about 5.00 am, these boys went round the neighbourhood, knocking at the doors of their relatives and friends, waking them up. For the amused audience, mostly still in pyjamas and nightdresses, two of the boys unfolded the scroll and recited in a kind of singsong the following rhymes, while the youngest among them would lie down to act the dead Lazarus. These are the lines I remember:

> Greet the well-known poor Lazarus
> Who is praised with voice and music.
> The long blessed fast is at an end,
> And Palm Sunday has come.
> The almond, the pomegranate are in leaf,
> And so is the fig-tree.
>
> Mary and Martha to him came
> With broken hearts and tears streaming
> Master! Hast thou with us stayed
> Our brother would not have died
> Nor in the grave had been interred.
>
> Weep not and wipe your tears
> Your brother will now arise.
>
> Lord have mercy on us and on our churches.
> Lord have mercy on all creatures.
> Thou who art our Saviour.

While the family studied the scroll of drawings, the boys would say, 'He who loves Christ, give us an egg.' Then the youngest boy would get up, having been brought back to life.

My father, who loved watching them, used to talk to them, teasing them and asking them to explain their artwork: 'First, show me who is this. Who is that beside Mary and Martha?' 'That's the neighbour.' 'That must be Lazarus in his wrappings, but look, his feet are showing.' They would smile shyly, take the eggs and hurry off as fast as they could. The art varied from crude to sophisticated, but all would have the same main features and characters – Jesus, Mary, Martha and Lazarus, women and men, a cross, trees, and a grave.

By now another party would have arrived. Sometimes you had two or three together in your house, some chanting, some rolling up their scrolls, others unfolding them. My brother would be out with one or two of his cousins, chanting to neighbours and collecting eggs. Usually by eight o'clock the drama was over. The boys would be in the alleys or playing at each other's homes, cracking their eggs, their scrolls discarded, while mothers prepared for another act of the divine drama – Palm Sunday.

For Palm Sunday, my mother would send my sister and me to her Greek Catholic cousins to get flowers for the candles – tall, thick candles with Christian symbols painted or carved on them, and decorated with beautiful satin ribbons. My mother's cousin Shafik lived in the Latin quarter with his family and his two aunts, Wardeh and Rujeina. We had to climb steps on the steep road to get to the house.

A path ran between the two sections of the garden which was typical for any Nazarene or, for that matter, any Palestinian garden. The Arabic name is *hakoura*. This is neither an orchard nor simply a flower-garden, as there are usually some fruit trees – lemon, apple, apricot, almond, pomegranate, olive, fig. Vines grow on bars or wooden planks so that the family can sit under it, in the sun. There are hedges formed out of jasmine, roses, stocks, lilies, and rosemary bushes. Vegetables and herbs – especially mint and parsley – are grown, including basil, tomatoes, spring onions and lettuce. The front of the house has a patio with pots of flowers, usually geraniums.

My sister and I were always warmly welcomed by all members of the family – Uncle Shafik and his wife had two daughters and three sons. The first to see us used to announce to the others, 'The daughters of Adma have come.' If my father happened to hear them say this, he would say jokingly, 'So they are Adma's daughters, not 'Aref's.' They would sit us down and give us lemonade, then take us to the garden to gather fresh scented flowers – roses, carnations and lilies, with rosemary and basil – and mint, spring onions, lemons and parsley from their kitchen garden. We would give them the message about which day of the week we would be making Easter cakes and they would promise to come and help. When we arrived home, carrying bouquets of flowers, as well as the herbs and vegetables, my mother was delighted and set about preparing the candles, arranging the flowers round them and tying them with pink or blue ribbons.

Uncle Shafik had a shop in the spice market of Nazareth which I remember visiting. Like other spice shops, it had jute sacks full of spice or heaps of different spices in big glass bowls. Shafik was the most honest man in the world, very fair in complexion with white hair, even though he was not very old. A small man, with back trouble, he used to explain in a very slow and patient manner about his herbs and spices – how each was good for treating different ailments: camomile, marjoram, rosemary, thyme, bayleaf, and pepper, cinnamon, nutmeg, cardamom and cumin. His hobby was reading old books and he was always concerned about my mother, asking after her health.

The Palm Sunday service was held in the afternoon, in the Greek Orthodox church. Families arrived, with children in their best attire, babies carried by their fathers or mothers, and somebody carrying the decorated Palm Sunday candles. It was such a popular feast that everybody came, including Muslims. The great attraction was the procession three times round the church – the *dora* (going round in a circle). Because of the lack of space, many would wait outside until the service finished. When the clergy emerged through the small doorway with their crosses and banners, everybody filed behind them, candles lit, ribbons fluttering, babies on the backs of their proud fathers, young girls beaming in their fine dresses, mothers trying to see how their daughters looked in comparison with other girls, handsome young men. The weather was usually fair but even if a shower of rain fell, it did not spoil the procession or daunt the candle-bearers.

You could not mention Easter in my town – or in virtually any other Palestinian or Lebanese town – without including

Easter cakes. My mother used to tell me that when she was young, people who owned land would allot a part of it for corn to be ground for the Easter cakes. Making them was a rather complicated job as any small mistake in the ingredients, the recipe or the baking could result in a catastrophe that might spoil the whole feast. Most families used between seven and eight kilos of flour and six to eight kilos of semolina. The cakes lasted for weeks and some were given away. The butter had to be pure and all the other ingredients – the flour, dates, walnuts or pistachios, nutmeg, cloves, cinnamon and gum arabic – had to be fresh so that the cakes tasted as good as possible.

Holy Week was very special. Every evening we went to *khatan* (evensong), a beautiful service marking the last week of Jesus' earthly life. Maundy Thursday was called the 'Reading of the Twelve Gospels', meaning the chapters that tell of the suffering and the trial of Jesus. Good Friday was called 'Sad Friday' in Arabic, when the scenes of the Passion were acted out and mournful chants sung. Everybody fasted and older women and bereaved families made a point of attending church in black clothes. The Greek Orthodox service started at 3.00 pm, when they acted out the gospel narrative of the crucifixion. The Christians of Nazareth, like all congregations of ancient churches, were always greatly moved by the Byzantine chants that described the different characters of the story. Many of these chants were composed by the eighth-century Arab theologian St John the Damascene:

Today is hung on a piece of wood
He that hung the earth on the waters.
A crown of thorns was put on the forehead of the King of
    Angels
And he that veiled the heavens with the clouds
Was dressed in a mock robe.
He that freed Adam in the Jordan was hit on the face.
The Bridegroom of the Church was nailed,
The Son of the Virgin was pierced with a spear.
We worship your suffering, O Christ.
Show us your glorious resurrection.

Joseph and Nicodemus prepare the body
That is clothed with Life.

Light of my eyes, my beautiful Son,
How were you veiled in a grave?

(*At this point rose water was sprinkled on the coffin carried by some of
the worshippers*)

Women carrying spice came early to your grave
To pour the perfume.
Grant by your resurrection peace to the church
And to the peoples salvation,
Now and forever, amen.
Prepare your servants, O Virgin,
For the sight of the resurrection of your Son.

The chants had a powerful effect on the listeners, making
them live the drama. I was always very moved by them. I also
went to the Anglican Good Friday service of Meditations on
the Cross and sang 'O Sacred Head', so being exposed to
another experience.

Saturday was called 'Saturday of the Sacred Fire or Light',
and the climax of Easter was the midnight service on that day,
when the bells of the Greek Orthodox church rang, heralding
the most glorious moment of the Christian calendar. My
mother used to wake us up. It was difficult at first, being fast
asleep, to leave a warm bed, but the pealing bells lured us. We
dressed up and joined other families on their way to the
church.

Sometimes I would go in and sit with my girl friends, filled
with awe as the dim lights shed long shadows on the old icons,
icons which showed women frantic with grief as the body of
Christ was taken down from the cross, and saints with long
beards, their grave, pale faces contrasting with their gorgeous,
gold-patterned habits. The Virgin Mary stared from other
icons, serene and sad.

We watched the churchwarden as he stood by the door.
There came a frantic knocking. The bishop, with the priests,
the acolytes and the whole community behind him, hammered
confidently on the heavy iron door, crying out, 'Open the doors
of eternity so that the King of Glory will enter.' 'Who is this
King of Glory?' the warden asked. The claim was repeated.
Then the doors opened. Triumphantly, bearing candles and

incense, the bishop and clergy entered the church, singing, 'Christ is risen from the dead, trampling death by dying, granting life to all who are in the grave. *Christus Anasti* (Christ is risen).' Then the service continued. Afterwards, we all joined in the procession going round the church three times, chanting 'Christ is risen, trampling death by dying.' One choir after another joined in canon until the music became a compulsive beat that pounded through your veins. Your heart swelled, something mystical took hold of you, and a great joy overwhelmed you.

Above, the stars were retreating. The first rays of the sun heralded the dawn and the sun rose, as if joining the procession of worshippers, a symbol of the Son of Righteousness. We lingered as the day broke. Who could take the joy of Easter from me or, for that matter, from any Middle Eastern Christian?

Back home, we breakfasted on Easter eggs and special bread, with fresh cottage cheese, strained yoghurt with olive oil and thyme, and a variety of jams. Then men, not women, started their visits of greeting, first to the elderly and the sick in the family and then to the brothers and cousins. Our house was filled with many relatives greeting one another with 'Christ is risen' in Arabic, the answer being 'Risen indeed'. Sometimes they found my father at home, sometimes he had already gone out to greet them and their families, like an exchange game. Muslim friends also came to greet us, as well as friends from other Christian denominations. The mothers served Arabic coffee and piles of Easter cakes on beautiful glass plates, as well as trays of chocolates, sugared almonds, pistachios, and preserved fruits bought specially from Damascus. Everybody was in their best clothes, little boys in navy or wine velvet suits, with silk shirts trimmed with lace, and the girls in the frilly summer dresses in pink or blue. Such dresses were acquired painstakingly, choosing the material, pattern, dressmaker and accessories. There were also new shoes, stockings, hats, gloves and bags to match the chosen dresses. Men wore new suits and white shirts.

If there were many family members for Easter lunch, a whole lamb was killed. The kidneys, liver and heart were grilled and eaten the evening before, usually with *'arak* (ouzo). The lamb was stuffed with rice, minced meat, pine nuts and sometimes almonds, as well as lots of spices. A soup was also served, with meat balls, rice, pine nuts and parsley.

If anyone had been bereaved, relatives would have sent them some cakes a few days before; a bereaved family would never make Easter cakes since these were a symbol of the joy that they were not entitled to share. They stayed in their black mourning clothes and only attended church on Good Friday. My mother used to send me with a box or two of Easter cakes to bereaved relatives and neighbours. At first they refused to take them, and I had to persuade them, saying, 'They are for the children. They should not miss the chance of tasting them while the other children are all eating them . . .'

School came as an anti-climax after the joys and festivities of Easter; as the proverb has it, 'The feast with its joy is gone, the teacher with his rod has come.' But I had had a wonderful time – two lots of festivities for Easter, because I went with my mother to all the Anglican services as well as the Orthodox ones. I knew some of the hymns by heart, some of them translated by my uncle Elias and included in our hymnbook, such as 'Here comes the conquering hero', and 'Lo, in the grave he lay'. My mother's Anglicanism was very important to her. It was the source of her joy and outlook on life and she considered it as one aspect of the renaissance of the Arab Christian world.

Summer Celebrations

Two more feasts awaited us after Easter – Ascension and Pentecost. They were official religious holidays when we did not go to school. Instead, we went on picnics either as a family or as a church group. Our church used to take us to Tiberias or to the woods. One feast which was only observed in Nazareth was called the Feast of Precipitation. You would think that the people of Nazareth would rather forget the episode:

When the people in the synagogue heard this, they were filled with anger. They rose up, dragged Jesus out of the town, and took him to the top of the hill on which their town was built. They meant to throw him over the cliff, but he walked through the middle of the crowd and went his way. (Luke 4. 28–30)

In the afternoon of the feast day, young men and women in summer clothes walked up the steep rocky hill on the south side of Nazareth overlooking the plain of Esdraelon. It was the season of green almonds and the walkers would take some with them as they climbed up and back – regretting what was done to Jesus, I hope.

The Feast of the Transfiguration came on 6 August. Mount Tabor, with its unique bell-shape, was part of the Nazareth landscape, one of the sites where tradition has it that the transfiguration took place. Many Nazareth people flocked to celebrate the feast on the mountain top. The road to the summit had many hairpin bends and before the coming of the car, people went up there on horseback. In later years, some would drive as far as they considered safe and then walk up the winding road.

Once you were on top of the mountain, you felt truly transfigured by the beauty of the landscape. You looked out on the plain, a carpet of many colours. Some people would pitch tents and bring out a *durbakeh* (a conical hand-drum). They sat in circles, singing, clapping, dancing to the rhythm of the *durbakeh*. There were two churches on the plateau at the top of the mountain, one for the Latin monks and the other for the Greek Orthodox. Both had hostels where people could stay. When I went to Mount Tabor, I was enchanted by the view, by the changing colours of the horizon where the purple and blue mixed, by the exquisite colours of the plain. I felt elated, as if I was really in a different world. That is why I am tempted to believe that the Transfiguration really did take place there, although the view from Mount Hermon (where it is also suggested that the Transfiguration happened) is breathtaking and more splendid. But I think that Galilee was Jesus' world: he often saw the dome-shaped mountain from the hills of Nazareth and would take his disciples with him to such a place that was unique and yet accessible.

4
Early
Awakenings

In my final years at primary school, I became aware of the troubles in my country, the open rebellion of the Palestinians against the pro-Zionist policies of British rule. There were demonstrations and strikes. The girls in my school stayed away, protesting against Jewish immigration and the Balfour Declaration. When I was in the top class, I joined them. We started from the square of the Greek Orthodox church, where the boys also assembled, and walked down the main street, passing the Latin convent, to the bus station, where we were joined by men and women from the surrounding villages, wearing their *kaffiyehs* (headscarfs). We sang about our homeland:

> This homeland, this homeland
> Deserves to be redeemed by our blood and hearts.
> Shame on us if we slumber and lose a right
> Which we should preserve.
> Rise up, rise up.
> Even if we suffer hardships
> By our own hands we shall redeem
> This homeland, this homeland.

Such marches became bigger and more organized. Even as very young people we felt anger at the injustice that we felt was being done to our people. The Palestinians were vulnerable and the government that was mandated to help them get their independence seemed to be against them; we felt that our country was being given away to immigrant Jews coming from all over the world.

By the end of the year, amid these difficult circumstances, I sat the entrance exam for the Women's Training College (WTC). To win a place was an honour, an acknowledgement of intelligence. Only fifteen girls were accepted from all the government schools of Palestine, after strict written and oral exams, so I was thrilled when I received the letter of acceptance and my mother perhaps even more so. Because of the troubles in Palestine – the general strike of May 1936 – we could only start in the second term which meant that I missed much of the basics in secondary education, especially in geometry and algebra.

The college proved a disappointment. Many people romanticize their school days, but not me. The colonial system was observed to the minutest detail and the English teachers tended to view the girls with disdain. I remember our music teacher, whom I shall call Miss L, turning to the piano at the start of the lesson, seeing dust on it, and saying, 'You Arabs can't do anything, even dust a piano.' We rebelled, and shouted back, then were punished by being made to go up and down the stairs many times, as well as having to write an apology.

It was at the college, however, that I discovered how much I liked psychology, as well as history and literature; there was also a lot of emphasis on handiwork – sewing, drawing and home economics – although I did not care for it much at the time. My insatiable desire was to read and learn, both in English and Arabic. The great Arab writers, such as Taha Hussein, Al Mazini, Tawfiq el Hakim, 'Abbas M. al-Aqqad, were very popular then, and reading and discussing their works was a growing trend of Palestinian cultural life, as well as reading the Lebanese writers who had founded another school of thought – Gibran Khalil Gibran, Michael Nu'aimeh. But there was little time for reading, because we had to help with the housework as well. I used to enjoy the afternoon when we had an hour and a half to play or eat whatever we had brought from home in the way of cakes or cheeses. I spent the time reading and learning by heart Arabic poetry which had enthralled me since I was quite small.

Our parents' visits kept us in touch with what was happening to our country, albeit in a vague way. The girls came from all parts of Palestine, so we heard news from further afield than might otherwise have been the case. We knew about the Arab Higher Committee, which included leaders of all five Palestinian parties and which had called the general strike of 1936. We heard about the great rebellion against the British which began in May that year, when the Mandate Government had to bring in military reinforcements from Malta and Egypt. In August the guerrilla leader Fawzi el-Qawuqji entered the country at the head of 150 volunteers from Arab countries to aid the uprising.

My friends and I argued about the extension of the general strike that went on for six months. I knew what difficulties the strike caused in Nazareth, with no shops open and the people just sitting around feeling angry and frustrated, refusing to accept the authority of the Mandate which had plans to uproot them from their Palestine. The Arab Higher Committee (the highest Palestinian politician body, established in April 1936 to co-ordinate resistance to Britain's pro-Zionist policies), presided over by the Mufti of Jerusalem, eventually accepted appeals from the Kings of Saudi Arabia and Iraq and the Emir of Transjordan to call off the strike on the understanding that their mediation would solve the conflict.

Then there was the arrival of the Royal Commission under the chairmanship of Lord Peel, which stayed for nearly three months, from 11 October 1936 until 18 January 1937. Their report recommended the partition of Palestine into a Jewish state, with the Arab state incorporated into Transjordan, together with the forcible transfer, if necessary, of Palestinians out of the Jewish state. It sounded ruthless and was rejected by the Arab Higher Committee which issued their own solution, demanding an independent unitary Palestinian state 'with protection of all legitimate Jewish and other minority rights'. In August 1937, the World Zionist Congress in its turn decided to 'ascertain terms . . . for the proposed establishment of a Jewish state'. In September the Arab National Congress took place in Syria, attended by 450 delegates from Arab countries. It rejected the Peel partition scheme, demanded termination of the Mandate, an end to Zionist immigration and prohibition of the transfer of Arab lands to the Zionists. I remember how that conference boosted the morale of the Palestinians, but the whole situation was highly inflammatory; at school we considered the British staff part of the Mandate machinery, while they were probably just as suspicious of us as we were of them.

There was great anger amongst the Palestinians when, on 1 October 1937, the British dissolved the Arab Higher Committee and all Palestinian organizations. Five leaders were exiled and sent to the Seychelles, although the president of the Committee, Haji Amin al-Hussayni, escaped to Lebanon. It was obvious that the Mandate Government was intent on destroying Palestinian leadership.

I remember 1938 as the year a bomb was planted by the *Irgun* (a Zionist terrorist group) in a café in Haifa, killing twenty-four Palestinians and injuring thirty-seven; there were more bombs – on a bus in Jerusalem on 4 July, and in the melon market on 6 July. In June that year a British officer by the name of Orde Wingate organized Special Night Squads (SNS) composed of British and *Haganah* (Jewish defence forces) personnel to carry out raids against Palestinian villages. This angered the Palestinians and convinced them that the British planned to uproot them, not only by political means as a governing authority, but by supporting the Zionist plans in practical ways. Palestinians would often quote the proverb, 'If the judge is against you, to whom will you go with your plea?'

There were more conferences, more bombs, more Commissions. The outbreak of the Second World War in 1939 accelerated the guerrilla attacks. In that same year, Malcolm MacDonald, the Colonial Secretary, issued the White Paper offering conditional independence for a unitary Palestinian state after an interval of ten years and the admission of 15,000 Jewish immigrants annually for five years, with ongoing protection of Palestinian rights. With hindsight some felt we should have accepted, but it was refused by the Arabs and vehemently rejected by the Zionists.

During the war years of 1939–45, there was little Palestinian political activity, although Britain continued to outlaw the Arab Higher Committee. People were awaiting the implementation of the MacDonald White Paper on land acquisition and limiting Jewish immigration. Food disappeared from all the shops. Rations were meagre unless you were involved in black market trading. An Italian plane dropped bombs once or twice on Haifa and many left to live in Nazareth, but they did not stay long.

In my town, people were taking sides. The British treated them badly, and none of the promises about independence were fulfilled; some people wanted Germany to win, some Russia and others the Allies. 'Stalin will have Hitler's head', said one, while another would say, 'I am for England. It will give us our rights, you'll see. They started the whole thing (meaning the Palestine situation) and they're the ones who'll solve it. There must be a fair solution.'

Meanwhile at school, our letters home were censored by the teachers which got me into great trouble when I wrote to my parents, complaining about how I was made to wear my old brown coat and not my new blue one. Brown was the school uniform colour, but that year the school authorities had been lenient about colour. The letter, along with one of my friend's complaining of bad treatment, were translated into English and then taken to the highest authority in the school, Miss Ridler.

Miss Ridler was the inspector of the government schools in Palestine, as well as director of the WTC. She was very much feared by everybody – and by everybody, I mean the whole teaching force in Palestinian schools, all the pupils of those schools, all the WTC staff, workers and pupils, and even the Department of Education. The only creatures who did not fear her were her dogs. She had green eyes, reddish hair and a flushed face, and wore a fur coat in winter. We never saw her in school except at the end of term when she read out the marks or made an announcement if something wrong had happened. She would fix her unflinching eyes on you and make you feel personally guilty.

When she read our letters, Miss Ridler was furious and demanded to see us at supper-time. The whole school was hushed, as the assistant headmistress took us to Miss Ridler's residence which was on the first floor of one of the boarding-houses, overlooking a garden. None of the schoolgirls had been to it before and, most likely, none of the Arab teachers. The assistant headmistress inspected us to see if we were presentable and she herself put her hat on, although we were in the same compound as the boarding-house. She said that we had brought this on ourselves and should take the consequences bravely. It was then that the horrible idea of being expelled from school crossed my mind.

We set off behind the teacher, feeling as if we were going to be executed. We were made to wait outside while the assistant headmistress went in before us. When we were summoned, Miss Ridler was sitting in a big chair. There was a fire crackling in the grate, the light reflecting on her flushed face and green eyes and red hair. It was like a scene from a Wagner opera. She came quickly to the point: how privileged we were to be in such a college which hundreds of girls would do anything to enter. We had scorned the college and described it as a prison. 'A prison,' she repeated. 'A prison. How dare you? You needn't have come here. You will hear more from me later.'

We went back to the school where all the girls were sitting at supper, their food untouched. The next day they sent for my uncle Elias and he tried to explain how the Arabic in my letter could actually have a different, less abusive meaning. He asked me to write a letter of apology and I agreed to do so, although I did not want to, feeling that the punishment outweighed the crime – but how would my parents and my uncle have felt if I had been expelled? My friend refused to apologise and was punished by being excluded from the school for a long time – although I recall that she too eventually wrote an apology.

On returning home for my summer holidays in 1939, I noticed that my sister's eye was drooping. This worried me, but when I asked my mother, she said it might have been caused by a recent bout of 'flu. My sister was also having terrible headaches. By the time I graduated from college in 1940, she was in a bad way. My parents took her to see a specialist in Haifa who diagnosed a brain tumour.

The specialist did not tell my mother that Nuha did not have long to live; for a year my sister seemed to recover and we believed that the worst was over. She had always been like an angel in our house, quiet and sweet-natured, the one who would calm my father if he flew into one of his rages. One day, however, my sister felt unwell. My mother sent me to her cousins, Wardi and Rujina Srouje, to ask them to sit with her. It was a long way to their house. They asked me to wait for them to come, but I could not. I set off home again, my heart strangely heavy. Two hundred metres from our house, near some shops, I felt my knees giving way and a great sorrow and fear overwhelmed me. I started to run, my heart racing. At the door of our home stood my father, together with some other relatives. My sister had just died.

I remember very little of what followed, except my father holding me. Nuha was laid out in the hall and our relatives were arriving, wailing and crying. My mother asked them to sing a hymn. We were devastated, but we kept the news from my brother because he was sitting his exams. When he finally came home and asked after Nuha and heard the news, his face grew so pale that even my mother, so upset herself, had to comfort him, saying things like 'It's better this way'.

5
Starting
Out

I was glad to graduate from school. There was nothing joyful about our graduation, though, because the Second World War was at its height, dominating everybody's thoughts and destinies. The future looked bleak. In Miss Ridler's farewell speech, she told us not to hope that we would all get jobs, which was unusual because WTC girls had never had problems in finding work in the past. Now we had to take what we could find.

At first I did not manage to get a job and felt very sorry for myself, but one day the headmaster of the local boys' school came to my father, with a letter from the Department of Education containing the news that there was a vacancy for a part-time teacher in Tiberias which I could take if I wanted, although he advised against it. My father was inclined to agree with him, but when he told me about the offer, I insisted on going. At least it was work. It was far worse than I had expected. I had to teach kindergarten, which was not what I was trained for, and I had to live with another teacher. Although she was kind and tried to help, I could not adapt to her routine. Every Friday, I went back to Nazareth, returned to work on Saturday morning and went home again for Sunday. Transport was difficult because of the war and sometimes I had to wait a long time for the taxi to fill with passengers.

Early on Mondays, at 5.00 am, I had to wait for the ride back to Tiberias, nervous that I might be late for work, hating the thought of returning to a town where I knew nobody. Even as the taxi started to descend the winding road towards Tiberias, I would feel claustrophobic and depressed. The lakeside beach of black, volcanic stones did not inspire me and the heat was intolerable. How different it might have been if I had had friends.

My salary was meagre and I hated standing in line to receive it, getting half what my colleague got although I had better qualifications. Perhaps they thought I had failed my exams. I could not resign, because that would end my career as a government teacher. I lost my appetite and was overcome with a host of fears; I was still grieving after my sister's death which had left the world feeling so empty. One Monday morning, I was on duty and so arrived earlier than usual from Nazareth. A little girl stood by the school gate with her friends. 'Please,' she said, 'Please excuse Elaine from school today.' 'Why?' I asked. 'She is dead,' chorused the girls. I did not know whether to laugh or cry. It turned out that there had been a wedding on Sunday afternoon. Spectators were standing on a balcony to see the bride and the balcony collapsed, killing several people including Elaine.

I was looking forward to the summer holidays and for the first three days I was all right, but then I collapsed. I could not eat as much as a single mouthful, and was rapidly becoming anorexic, although the term was not widely known then. My mother prepared delicacies to tempt me to eat and watched anxiously as I struggled and failed to swallow anything. At night I felt as if I was drowning and I was afraid and restless, so that my mother had to stay by my side. The doctor gave me strong doses of barbiturates because I could not sleep.

I was terrified by what was happening to me. When I felt well, I was happy, elated, and then suddenly I would plunge into despair. If it were not for the support of my parents, I would have sunk into God knows what abyss. My mother sat beside me, dismissing my fears about myself, my depression: 'We all get depressed. You should have seen me when I was your age.' Or: 'It is the autumn. You know how the seasons affect us. It will all pass one day and you will tell your children about it.'

When my father came home from his clinic he tried to comfort me: 'What is it now? Let it go. Live free!' 'But I can't,' I would say. 'I want to fulfil myself. I want a way of life that is different.' He used to quote Al Muttanabi: 'Take whatever course you wish – that of life or death.' He told me the story of the Persian shah who, if he was happy, was overjoyed. If he was sad, he would be overwhelmed by sadness. He asked for help from his wise men but they could not find a cure. Then one day one of them gave him a tile on which was written: 'Every situation passes away'. The king had the tile hung on his wall. When he was overjoyed, he would look at the tile and slow down, and when he was sad, he did the opposite.

Sometimes I would be myself again and for a fleeting moment I would say to myself, 'I am all right. All is well.' But by the time I had told myself that my fears were foolish, the despair, the sense of strangeness had crept back. My mother took me to Haifa to see a doctor. He said I was on the verge of a nervous breakdown caused by anorexia. He prescribed medicine and said I must take life easy. It was like any other physical disease, but I had to remember to eat. It took me a long time to get better.

Leaving Home

My brother Irfan was the youngest in our family. Three years younger than I, he was good-looking, very sharp and intelligent. All through his primary and secondary schooling he came first in every subject and in 1940 he won a place at the Arab College in Jerusalem. A Mr Farrell was director of the Department of Education at the time. As a classicist, he was keen on introducing Latin and Greek to Middle Eastern students and chose my brother for private lessons. Later, with two other bright students, Irfan travelled to England to spend a year at Durham University studying Greek and Latin and then went on to St John's College, Oxford.

My brother's departure saddened my father, although he was proud of him. I still remember going with him to Haifa to say goodbye at the railway station, where he was catching the train with his friends to Port Said and from there a ship to England. My brother's most important possessions were his books and he carried those with him to England via Egypt. As the train moved off, my brother trying to wave to us, my father, mother and I ran after it. My father never saw my brother again.

It was very sad returning home without Irfan. As we approached the Kawar quarter, our relatives looked down from their balconies and windows at us. Later, when they came to visit, they would say to my mother, 'We never saw 'Aref so stooped and depressed as when he returned after saying goodbye to Irfan. He looked a broken man.' They all thought that my brother should marry, settle down and continue the family line, especially as he was the only son. When, after having coffee, visitors to our house would say the customary phrase

'*Daimeh*' ('May your coffee always be served', which implies continuity), followed by 'May we drink it at your son's wedding!', my father would answer, 'Where will I be then? In the grave?' 'God forbid, Abu Irfan! Why do you speak like this?' the visitor would say. '*Inshallah* (God willing) he will come back, you will marry him off and play with his children on your lap.' My father would nod his head, unbelieving. His gloom was dispelled only by the arrival of Irfan's letters which turned an ordinary day into a feast, he always said.

New Directions

I was teaching in Nazareth by this time, as well as comforting my parents. They needed me every minute, not so much for practical help as for boosting their morale. I longed to go for further education, but could not think of leaving them. Besides teaching, I busied myself with many other activities. I taught at the Anglican Sunday School, joined the YWCA and the Girl Guides, wrote and staged plays, and became very active with the British Council, translating speeches into Arabic.

One day I received an invitation to speak at the Greek Orthodox club in Haifa. Greek Orthodox clubs were very successful as the indigenous community, denied the right to lead their churches by the Greek Patriarchate, expressed their identity in their cultural life by founding schools and clubs. The Haifa Club was a very prestigious place and I spoke to a full house for an hour and a half, to mounting enthusiasm from the audience. In my speech I drew attention to what I felt was wrong in our society and in education, stressing the lack of status for women, the neglect of Arabic language, history and culture, and the need for discipline in a society that was facing the threat of Zionism. I closed by addressing the Palestinian question: 'In your *jihad* [struggle] for Palestine, you have to discipline yourselves. If you are negligent, you will lose Palestine. Your exodus will be more tragic than when you were thrown out of Spain. For the exodus from Spain was from a foreign country, but the exodus from Palestine is from the heartland of our Arab world. If you do not struggle, you will be like those whom the Caliph Ali addressed after the battle of Anbar: "How diligent are those in their unjust claim and how failing you are in what is your right."'

I received a standing ovation, but the next day I was ordered by my headmaster to present myself to the Department of Education inspectors to give an account of what I had said. One of the strict rules for all government employees was that they should not be involved in politics. This law was one of the most subtle and subversive weapons used by the Mandate Government to thwart the efforts of the Palestinians to express themselves. It had a psychological effect, stifling the personality of government employees, making them inhibited, secretive and over-cautious, because anybody caught dabbling in politics was immediately fired from their job.

Once government employees, who constituted the bulk of educated Arab Palestinians, had been marginalized, there was nobody left to speak out except the peasants and the landowners, traders and the few who had their own little businesses. What was it they called 'politics'? It was our destiny – we were watching our country being sold off. To add insult to injury, the law did not apply to the Zionists. As far as my Greek Orthodox club speech was concerned, I was allowed to get away with my political comments because I had raised mostly social issues – and it may have been that the department inspector himself agreed with what I had said.

I started to write to the Palestine Broadcasting Station (PBS) and was overjoyed when my first talk was accepted. Later I became a regular contributor with pieces for the schools programme, and the women's programme, with plays, talks and, most importantly for me, short stories. I was also writing for the Near East Broadcasting station, for the Arabic section of the BBC, and also for the Hilversum broadcasting station in Holland. Some of my friends and acquaintances were already broadcasters or heads of stations, and I would sometimes be asked to write for them.

Those two years from 1946 to 1948 were happy ones for me as a young writer. I looked forward every morning to the postman bringing me a published article or story, or a request to write in a magazine, an invitation to speak, and sometimes a little money from the PBS or BBC World Service. What I liked writing best was the prose poem, a literary form which was becoming increasingly popular, led by the Lebanese school and the Poets of the Diaspora (the Arab-American poets such as Gibran Khalil Gibran). Many of my prose poems were published, especially in a number of Lebanese literary magazines which began asking me to write for them, and in the Palestinian magazines *Al Qafilah* and *Al Mihmaz*. I even received an invitation to write for a magazine in Iraq.

The PBS had three sections – Arabic, English and Hebrew. Everyone worked together in the same building. We loved our Arab broadcasters, getting to know them by their youthful, clear voices which gave us courage and confidence. Among them were Musa Dajani, 'Aqil Hashim, Raji Sahyoun, 'Isam Hammad and Fatima Budairi. The PBS building in Jerusalem belonged to the Anglican Church and the vicarage stood next to it. My uncle, Canon Elias Marmura, lived there with his family, and the young broadcasters got to know him and his older children who were by then university students. They would drop in occasionally and the conversation would be academic and scholarly, as my uncle was well versed in Arabic culture.

My uncle was aware of the importance of recording Palestinian tradition and culture, and suggested collecting Palestinian folk tales. The idea was put to the head of PBS, Mr 'Azmi Nashashibi, and the call went out for listeners to send in the tales they knew. I contributed three tales, but the whole programme did not last long, for terrible events awaited us. They were events that ended the most beautiful tale of all – the tale of life in Palestine – and destroyed my uncle's home, crushed our dreams and turned us into refugees. It was like entering a dark tunnel, finding, like generations of our families before us, that the land which we had loved and where we had been born was to be usurped, snatched from beneath our feet under all kinds of pretexts and that this wrongdoing was supported by the most powerful states in the world.

6
The Legacy
of War

It was 22 July 1946 and together with three Nazareth friends I was attending a Girl Guides' training camp in Ramallah for leaders from all over Palestine. We were enjoying ourselves, learning woodcraft and other skills, and looking forward to a stage show and party on the last day. There were a few British participants and relations with them were generally pleasant and friendly until terrible rumours began to spread through the camp: the King David Hotel, location of the government offices, had been bombed.

Everybody was frightened, Palestinian and British alike. We all had either close family, relatives or acquaintances who might have been affected. We tried to carry on as normal, however, until the camp was over. Then, already burdened with the tragedy awaiting us, we went home to learn that the *Stern*, a Jewish terrorist group, headed by Menachim Begin, had put bombs in the milk containers that were brought to the hotel, killing 101 people.

It was at this time that the idea was put forward that I should be put in charge of Women's Affairs for the PBS, because I was already a regular contributor. I loved the idea of such a job, as I found that teaching was taking me away from the creative work which I liked most of all. The national situation was deteriorating, however. The partition resolution of 29 November 1947 recommended the creation of a Jewish state, but the Arabs refused to accept it and the violence between the different sides rapidly worsened.

By the time I got the letter confirming my PBS appointment and inviting me to Jerusalem, the shootings and the bombings and the dreadful shadow of all-out war made me think twice about accepting. Also my father's health was giving great cause for concern. Amongst other symptoms, he was suffering from enlargement of the heart and high blood pressure and he had not been well enough to attend the funeral of my uncle Elias who had died in May that year. He suddenly began to grow weaker and fell into a coma, although he regained consciousness for a while and still managed to show his sense of humour. Seeing the crowd of relatives and friends sitting round him, he said aloud to himself, 'Shame on you, 'Aref! All these people are waiting for you to die and you can't do it!' Everybody in the room was so embarrassed, trying to hide their smiles at such a sad and anxious time. He spent a whole week in this state, hovering between life and death. Then one day, mid-morning, he died.

In no time our house was crowded with our many relatives, but to me everything was silent. A great soul had departed and I felt the loss like a heavy weight on my back. My mother was in a state of collapse. Her health had always been weak and the death of my father reduced her to helplessness. As was customary in those days, my father was laid in the hall of the house and the women mourners surrounded the body while the men were received in the sitting-room. The women began singing dirges and my mother and I sat and wept. I can still remember the rhythm of the songs, accompanied by a certain way of clapping, where the hands swayed from side to side. Some of the songs represented the deceased asking the living to buy him back from death, with the living offering to give the most precious thing, such as a Yemeni sword in a jewel-decked sheath. There was nothing that broke the heart and brought tears to the eyes so much as those dirges sung in unison, in the saddest of voices. Even as I write this down, remembering, my eyes fill with tears and I have to leave my writing to do something else.

For forty days after the funeral, people visited to pay their condolences, as was customary, and our closest relatives stayed with us for the first few days, helping us receive the visitors who included representatives from the whole town. Being visited, sharing our grief and talking about my father, helped to dispel the shadow of death and gradually prepared us for a new life without him.

Meanwhile the news of the war grew worse. I was still receiving letters about the PBS job, and now I decided to take my chance. My extended family begged me not to go to Jerusalem, but my suitcase was packed and one afternoon I decided to ignore all their pleas and go. My mother came with me and on the way we met a friend. Seeing my suitcase, she asked where we were going and I had to explain. She turned to my mother: 'Um 'Irfan, your daughter is young and adventurous, but aren't you older and wiser? How can you allow her to do this?' I did not listen to her warnings. At the garage we again met people who tried to dissuade us. One man, another friend of our family, was waiting there for the bus from Jerusalem. His sister was coming home from boarding school on it, because her family had decided it was not safe for her to stay in the Jerusalem area. 'Please,' he said to me. 'My advice is that you really should not go.' Nevertheless we waited for the bus which was due from Haifa, passing through Nazareth on the way to Jerusalem. It never arrived. It had been fire-bombed and burnt out on the way – the last bus to travel between north and south.

It seemed like a sign from God that the job was not right for me. I returned home with my mother, and later wrote a letter of resignation from the job I never held. After writing the letter, I held back from signing it for days, just in case, but the bombing and gunfire was worsening and now targeting the PBS itself. The situation was hopeless. I signed the letter and sent it.

To add to our woes at this time, the emergency laws of the British Mandate left us not only defenceless but a target for harassment. How many times did we hear of the inhabitants of a Palestinian village forced out of their houses, the men made to squat in the sun like naughty children, while the army searched for arms, throwing around their winter provisions, their olive oil, their wheat, and frightening the women and babies? Woe betide the people of that village if the army found so much as a rusty pistol. Houses were destroyed, men rounded up and imprisoned, curfews imposed.

The destruction of the 'Awn Allah residence opposite our own Nazareth home left a terrifying, lasting impression on me. It was a massive building belonging to a well-known Muslim family, with lofty, vaulted rooms, two flights of stairs and a big hall. Under the emergency laws, it was decided to destroy this building. I cannot remember what the reasons were, but I think it had something to do with weapons. It was an act which the whole city resented, seeing it as a symbolic crushing of the Palestinian leadership. I remember the residents of the surrounding houses being ordered out, so that the army could get to work on the house. I went with my parents to the home of one of my many uncles who lived at the top of one of the Nazareth hills. When we came back to our neighbourhood, we saw the majestic 'Awn Allah house turned into a heap of fallen stones. I still cannot describe our anger at the arbitrary powers which could so destroy the home of a generous and noble family – or, for that matter, the home of anybody.

Despite hearing that Winston Churchill had declared that the British would leave Palestine, along with its other colonies, and despite the deteriorating situation, my people could not quite bring themselves to believe what was happening. We sat for hours, arguing about what was going on, trying to find out from those working for government officials if they knew anything more. I knew many Palestinian employees in the Mandate Government who were carrying on with their jobs meticulously and faithfully, even as they saw their seniors packing up, leaving work unfinished and sending their families abroad ahead of them.

The Jewish lobby by then had moved from Britain to the United States. Palestinians came to believe that the US presidency was the decisive factor in the future of their country, rather than considerations of human rights or the suffering of a people. This became more evident as President Truman took a very hard line against the Palestinians in his election year. Since August 1945 Truman had called repeatedly for 100,000 Jewish immigrants to enter Palestine, on humanitarian grounds after the Holocaust. There was no offer of homes in America or any other countries for the persecuted Jews who had endured such terror and pain, suffering and death.

If the Balfour Declaration gave a national homeland to the Jews, the UN Partition scheme of 29 November 1947 heralded the final shattering of our hope by giving the Zionists what would be the larger share of the country. The Palestinians bitterly opposed the plan, considering it an outrageous idea when they were the indigenous people, owning 93 per cent of the land and making up 65 per cent of the population. Truman, however, put great pressure on the other UN member states to vote for the Partition plan. While the Zionists had a detailed strategy established for fulfilling their goal, the political expertise and financial resources of Jews all over the world, and the support of the former British Mandate and the present US Government, the Palestinians had nothing except promises from the Arab League, their own fighters and the support of a number of voluntary groups from some of the Arab countries. For the most part, however, they still had too much faith in British fairness and justice. They could not believe that the West could allow a whole people to be turned out of their country.

The month of November has a bad reputation with the Palestinians, often ushering in 'the winter of our discontent'. The Balfour Declaration was on 2 November 1917. The UN General Assembly passed a resolution recommending the Partition of Palestine on 29 November 1947. In the aftermath of that day, there was a long sequence of tragic events: cities fell, villages were destroyed and populations fled; there was bloodshed, poverty, anger, defeat, and thousands of tents housing disillusioned, dispossessed people, who were innocent of any wrongdoing except the love of their country, and their desire to return to it and continue their ordinary lives as ordinary human beings. These were people who were later stigmatized as terrorists and infiltrators.

Partition

In spite of the situation, I still went to school each day but my teaching was continuously interrupted when pupils did not turn up. Some parts of Palestine were now directly under Jewish authority and in many other parts fighting was still going on, with sniping, mortar shelling and rockets. We never knew whether to expect news of victory or defeat, and then one day we heard of the terrible events at Deir Yaseen and on the same day, the death of one of our heroes.

The village of Deir Yaseen lay on the western edge of Jerusalem. On the night of 9 April 1948, 250 men, women and children were massacred there in cold blood, many of them lying asleep in their beds. The murderers from the *Stern* and *Irgun* gangs (two Jewish terrorist groups who committed atrocities against British and Arab persons before the establishment of the State of Israel) were not satisfied with killing but went on to mutilate the bodies and cut open the bellies of pregnant women. The act horrified the Arab world and made the

Palestinians panic, leading to the exodus of whole populations from many cities and towns, fleeing in their thousands in the belief that the same fate awaited the rest of them.

The other tragic event of 9 April 1948 was the death of 'Abed el-Qadir el-Husseini, son of Musa Kazim Pasha el-Husseini who was appointed Mayor of Jerusalem after the British occupation of Palestine but later removed because he opposed pro-Zionist policies. His son Abd el-Qadir was looked on as a freedom fighter and was much respected and admired by his followers. He was killed in a counterattack on the Qastal hill (castle), six miles to the west of Jerusalem, in a strategic position on the mountains overlooking the Jerusalem–Tel Aviv road. The name of Abd el-Qadir was well known throughout Palestine and the news of his death cast a black shadow of despair over all of us. In Jerusalem thousands of people filled the streets, weeping. It was yet another setback to a people who needed strong leadership.

On 18 April 1948, the British withdrew suddenly from Tiberias, a city where Arab and Jew had lived peacefully together for many decades. For Nazareth people it was where we went on holidays because of its mineral baths, its many religious sites and the lake where we loved to swim. In the cool of the day we would sit by the lakeshore and eat the local catch, still known as St Peter's fish, watching the evening descend on the surrounding hills and the lights of the fishing boats, perhaps meditating on the Man of Nazareth who made the shores of the lake his home and sat in a boat to preach, telling stories and parables, and choosing fishers of men.

Following the British withdrawal from Tiberias, the Arab population panicked. Most fled to Syria and Jordan as the *Haganah* moved in. Some families came to Nazareth. My own aunt's family fled to Amman, never again to see their much-loved home with its long terrace and beautiful garden.

If the fall of Tiberias shocked us, the fall of Haifa on 22 April was a far worse blow. In Nazareth we had very close links with Haifa, as hundreds of our young men commuted to the coastal town to work in the refineries, the railway, the factories and the government departments, as well as their own businesses. Haifa was booming in the last years of the Mandate and many people went to live there, building their own houses on Mount Carmel or on the coast. To us in Nazareth, Haifa was modern and rich, another place for holidaymaking with its combination of sea and mountains. When we were in primary school, we knew by heart the three pillars of Haifa's importance. There was IPC, which stood for the Iraqi Petroleum Company – Haifa was the outlet for the pipes carrying the precious oil from Iraq; the refineries, like huge secular temples, stood there solemnly, belching out carbon dioxide, their noxious incense. Then there was the harbour where stately ships glided in, ringed by factories making cement, detergents, chocolate, biscuits, cigarettes. And there was the railway terminus, the last station on the line from Egypt.

Fighting started in Haifa immediately after the UN had passed the November 1947 resolution, and the violence escalated, with the Jewish and Arab quarters becoming like two enemy camps. Nazareth workers who were still commuting to the coast by bus (when they could) told horrific stories of Jews planting bombs in the vegetable market, killing 130 Palestinians, and the Arabs retaliating. The *Stern* and *Irgun* gangs increased their terrorist attacks and the Arab volunteer forces, mainly from Syria and Lebanon, could not equal the trained troops of the *Haganah*.

The sudden British withdrawal from Haifa was originally scheduled for August 1948, although it emerged that Zionists had been notified of an earlier date of withdrawal, of which the Arabs were unaware. Then, the ending of the Mandate was announced as 15 May 1948, and the British were ordered out of Haifa on 21 April – but the Arab exodus had already begun, following the massacre of Deir Yaseen. The people fled by any means they could find, in trucks, taxis, or by sea. On 22 April the *Haganah* took the city, attacking the Arab quarter ruthlessly, and people left in their thousands, abandoning their homes and going to the harbour, desperately looking for boats to ferry them to Lebanon, Gaza or Egypt. Many of those who fled were our friends, neighbours and relatives. In Nazareth I spoke to mothers, whose sons had left Haifa with their families, men, women and children thrown into ferries, heading to the unknown and leaving behind furniture, provisions, or whole businesses.

Jaffa had been the most important harbour in Palestine before the rise of Haifa, as well as being famous for its orange orchards. In the 1947 Partition plan, Jaffa was supposed to be situated in the Palestinian state, although it was surrounded by many Jewish settlements and was close to Tel Aviv. Early in December 1947 the fighting began, but the city did not have sufficient arms to defend itself. Chaos spread as the *Haganah* encircled the city on 25 April 1948. The people fled in their thousands, travelling by sea to Gaza or Egypt. Many drowned on the journey. The rich and proud city of Jaffa was left deserted, its renowned orchards left for the Zionists to occupy. With the fall of each Palestinian city, we felt increasingly vulnerable, stripped of beloved places.

By the end of April, most of the thriving, ancient Palestinian cities had fallen into the hands of the Zionists. The villages dotting the landscape with their slender minarets were ruined. More than half the civilian Arabs of Palestine had become displaced persons, houses were wrecked beyond repair and the people turned into refugees. On 14 May 1948, the British flag was lowered from the official residence in Jerusalem, as the High Commissioner, Sir Alan Cunningham, inspected a guard of honour for the last time, thus ending the British Mandate in Palestine.

7

Moving Rocks from Mountains

Jerusalem had been a target for terrorist attack since November 1947. The residential areas of the Arabs were attacked ruthlessly, all beautiful neighbourhoods with houses and villas built with the red-veined or blue-veined stones of Jerusalem. These areas fell after a long and bitter fight, and the inhabitants made their way to Ramallah and Bethlehem, forced from their beloved capital city, in one of the most horrifying scenes of the Palestinian exodus. Many crossed the Jordan to Amman, Salt and other cities. The northern part of Jerusalem, including the Old City, was saved by the heroism of its defenders and later by the intervention of the Arab legion of the Transjordan army on 19 May 1948.

We were specially concerned about my late uncle's family, wondering what had happened to them. Had they been spared the bullets and the shooting? Had they crossed the river and reached a safe haven? What about their house which had always been so welcoming, their beautiful garden with its huge pepper tree? Then we heard the news that they had had to flee to Jordan, in very difficult and dangerous circumstances, leaving their home. I felt as if a haven of my soul was gone forever.

Times were bad in Nazareth after the British had left. There was no government, although some local prominent families tried to handle our affairs. One day, my mother said to me, 'Najwa, I was sitting here in my bedroom and by the balcony door I saw a man standing in tattered clothes, with a very sad face. Then he disappeared. I think that he must have been Jesus. He is very sad about what is going to happen to us.' I believed my mother, not just because she was a devout Christian, but because it was not in her nature to imagine things. She must have experienced something real. It was true that Jesus was with us, sharing our sorrow, grieving for what the world was doing to the people of Palestine. As events grew worse, my mother would repeat her story, saying that she knew what was coming because of seeing that tattered man standing by the door, his face so sad.

In July 1948, our school broke up for the summer holidays, not knowing what the future would bring. We went home, our lives haunted by disbelief that what was happening or had happened was final. Many of the villages around Nazareth had fallen. The houses had been blown up and the inhabitants driven out. A continuous stream of refugees were arriving in the city and were housed in Christian institutions – convents, schools and hostels. The Latin boarding school, called appropriately *Abu al-Yatama* (Father of the Orphans), housed 600 refugees from the surrounding villages, with ten families to a room.

The hospitals were full of the wounded and sick. I used to walk past the Casa Nova, a Latin convent, where crowds of refugees had found shelter. There I got to know a woman originally from Tiberias who had been left on her own after the death of her mother. She used to visit us at home and would cry for her garden, talking about her plants as if they were human. When it was known that a nearby village was under attack, a cry of '*Najda! Najda!*' ('Help, help urgently') would go up and volunteers would set off with the few weapons they had. We would wait in suspense until they returned, taking the wounded to the hospitals, and the dead to a martyr's funeral.

One night in July, we heard tanks. In the very early hours of the morning a curfew was imposed and a fearful silence and gloom crept over the city. My mother and I thought it best to go to the house of one of my uncles, in spite of the curfew, and crept there by the shortest way. When we heard shooting begin, we decided to go to the vaulted hall below. This hall, one of the biggest in Nazareth, had originally been a sesame oil press for making *tahini* (sesame paste), built by my great grandfather, Tanous Kawar. It was dark, winter dark, in there and although it was not comfortable, you felt safe inside. The whole place felt ancient, far removed from our misery. 'I have seen and known the Turkish times, the British Mandate,' the walls seemed to say. 'Nothing will endure forever.'

Being together helped us while away the time. What were we waiting for? To be liberated? We could hear that all was quiet now, but it was an empty sort of quiet, a kind of nothingness. We decided to go upstairs. After an hour or so, our friend, neighbour and family doctor, Dr Jubran Attallah, came round. Full of confusion and desperately anxious, we begged him to tell us what was happening. 'It is finished,' he said. 'What has finished? Are the Arab armies in control?' we asked. He was a quiet man of few words and now he did not reply. We pressed him. At last he said, 'The city has surrendered.'

It was yet another story of a well-equipped, well-trained army, under British protection, and a disorganized force with old-fashioned weapons and dud ammunition. The Zionists passed through the main street of Nazareth in their army trucks, wearing the traditional Arab headgear of the *kaffiyeh* and *iqal* (plaited band) to conceal their identity. People with houses on the main road came out to greet them, assuming they were Arab troops. One woman, by the name of Miriam, began singing a song in praise of Fawzi el Qawqji, commander of the Arab Salvation Army. One of the passing army vehicles fired a bullet, hitting her in the neck and killing her. For three days, her body lay near Mary's Well. I sometimes wonder if she was spared knowing the truth before she died.

It is still hard to grasp what happened, let alone accept it, even now. Over the next few days we had to change our passports to Israeli identity cards, our money from Palestinian currency to Israeli which immediately became very low in value. Our city looked strange, with on the one hand thousands of refugees occupying every space available, and on the other hand armed women searching people under the powers of the new Israeli authorities. The Israelis immediately imposed military rule on all the Arabs. This meant that we had no redress to the civil courts and Arab land was seized. Travel between towns and villages was severely restricted because nobody could travel without a permit. Long lines of Arabs would have to stand for hours, waiting for a permit, only to be told that they had to come back the next day, simply in order to get to work or to see a doctor. People suffered imprisonment, house arrest, destruction of their homes, loss of employment, all without any possibility of going to a higher court to seek justice. Military courts had absolute powers and could justify all their judgements by the sacred word 'security'.

Aid in the form of food rations and second-hand clothes was handed out to refugees whose own lands were just a few miles away. I was on a team which distributed clothes and we found it hurtful to see completely unsuitable garments, such as corsets or hats, in these bales, sent to people who would never wear such clothing. It was pathetic to see them waiting for their rations or lining up in soup kitchens when their villages, now destroyed along with their beautiful vegetable and fruit gardens, had lain so close by.

It is still difficult to sum up my feelings at that time. Anger, disbelief, despair, loss. 'How can I go on from here? What have I become? Whom can we blame?' The calamity which had befallen us was worse than our darkest imaginings. A sense of gloom and emptiness fell on Nazareth which deepened my depression. The city was the embodiment of my shattered soul. The trees, the little gardens looked drooping and meaningless, the alleyways dull and hopeless. The people I talked to seemed dazed, unable to realize the enormity of what had happened. Most of them refused to believe that the situation would last: 'They can't throw a people out of their country, even if we were defeated.' 'Many peoples are conquered but they are not driven out of their homeland.' 'The UN would not allow it. We are in the twentieth century, after all.'

Again my mother stood by me. She told me – as she had told me before – how much they had suffered in the First World War, that they could have been killed on more than one occasion, that we could never know what tomorrow would bring. She started doing embroidery and I still treasure the beautiful tablecloth which she made at that time. 'Najwa!' she said, 'If we have to leave our home, we must make sure we take this tablecloth with us, even if we do not take anything else!'

I went on hating everything, even loathing myself because I felt that in some way the situation was my fault, that I could have done or said something to stop it happening. I remember one evening when I was walking by the Italian convent. Lights were shining from its many windows and the whole building looked peaceful and warm, unblemished by the misery of the moment. On another occasion I saw the lights shining from the Anglican church at evensong. Again I felt peace emanating from that place. Who was enjoying that peace? The answer came to me: those who belonged to Jesus. Shining like lamps, little unassuming lights. They had faith, something which nobody could take from them. I knew my faith was weak. I was no steadfast rock, I had doubts – yet I felt borne up by the faith which those others had. I felt it lifting my depression. I thought of Jesus, my friend. Jesus who was a carpenter and who walked up the hill after the day's work and sat on a rock and saw the landscape which I could still see. He would have sat in contemplation, united with God, free in spirit. He believed in life, he did not flee suffering but faced it.

It was the outcome of such thoughts which led me to the idea of reviving the YWCA in Nazareth, although previously it had not been well attended. It would be a coming-together of my townswomen which would help us live through our unhappy circumstances. I wrote to the YWCA headquarters in Geneva and talked to the members of the original Nazareth group. The Greek Orthodox church committee gave us permission to use their church hall and we began meeting twice a week. It was a success. After work we would hurry to the hall and prepare for a speaker or a bazaar. I started a drama group and we performed at Christmas and Easter. The thriving group encouraged me to think about having a YMCA as well and eventually I was instrumental in starting a branch in Nazareth.

By September 1948 the new authorities notified us that schools were to reopen, with the introduction of Hebrew as a subject. Many of us were finding the new circumstances difficult, but if we were to continue working and winning our daily bread, as well as teaching our children, we had to co-operate with the system. As soon as my school opened, the teachers were invited to a semi-official meeting in the home of one of the teachers' relatives. I felt hesitant, but went along anyway. When I arrived, I found some Jewish women there, invited by the hostess, besides other women from Nazareth. I chose to sit in an obscure corner, feeling restless and awkward, wishing I could have been more decisive and refused to come. An Arab woman was speaking to the audience, welcoming us. She spoke most kindly to the Jewish women, avoiding the one subject which was burning in all our hearts. The audience was unhappy, uncomfortable and in my back seat I was resigning myself to a wasted hour. When the speaker sat down, however, I suddenly heard my name spoken, called out from more than one direction. The other Arab women wanted me to speak for them, to express their anger, their despair, to speak about the injustice done to them.

Caught unawares, I had no idea what to say. I crossed the room, clinging to a few lines of poetry that crossed my mind, although not very relevant:

> To move rocks from the tops of mountains
> Is more to my liking than men's favours for me.
> Men say there is shame in work.
> The worst shame is the humiliation of begging.

I said, 'We are not pleading or begging. We simply want to remind you that we have a right to this country, to live in dignity and have our basic human rights.' The audience clapped, relieved. I elaborated on the point that women's rights could not be taken out of the context of basic human rights. The audience clapped again. One or two even cried. I sat down and received profuse thanks from my countrywomen. As the meeting closed, a young Jewish woman came up to me. She said she was impressed by what I had said and that she wanted to see more of me. She seemed intelligent and understanding, but I was not ready for that kind of contact. I wanted to go home, hide in a corner and cry, forgotten by the world.

A few weeks later, there was a conference on Arabic language and literature for both Jewish and Arab teachers, convened by Ben Ze'ev, a Jewish researcher in Semitic languages who at one time had lectured at Cairo University. As a teacher, I was asked to go along and speak on the Arab poet Al Muttanabi. The conference took place at the Government Girls' School which was packed out. Men and women from all walks of life came. It gave a disorientated city some kind of focus to hear their language and poetry, as well as spend time together, knowing that we all shared the same plight.

My lecture on Al Muttanabi was a success. Ben Ze'ev said he had not heard such a good presentation even in the university. I mentioned the poet's diction, the compelling music of his poetry, his powerful metaphors, his ability to identify himself with the ethos of the Arab and his ideals, his ability to express human experience in short verses that became proverbs, part of our daily repertoire. But had I done the right thing in taking part in such a conference? I met pleasant, intelligent Jewish men and women there – but could personal relationships erase the injustice done to my people? How could I carry on being true to what I believed to be right, as the face of my country and the social set-up changed so rapidly? In the end, I came to feel that a cultural relationship should only exist between equals because it would otherwise be a cover-up for the oppressor, a means of hiding the fact that lands and rights were being taken away.

In the seventeen years that I stayed in what became Israel, I met many Jewish people who impressed me with their integrity, but they were only a small part of a worldwide machinery with its own aims and systems, its savage onslaught on the Palestinian people, their land, their culture and their identity. The state constitution claimed equality, but the practice was different. Between 1948 and 1951 the government closed off whole areas of Arab land 'for security reasons'. Then in 1951 a law was passed saying that all land which had not been ploughed between 1948 and 1951 would be expropriated. The military governor simply gathered the inhabitants of a village together and said, 'Your land is expropriated'. With one dash, Israel crossed the names of the peasant owners off their registers. The Law of the Absentees was another shameful act. Many Palestinians remained in Israel as refugees from their villages and towns, either because of the shooting or because they happened to be away on business when the army arrived. These people were now declared absentees and lost their homes and their land.

I heard that there was to be a conference for the *Histadrut* (Jewish Workers' Union) in Tel Aviv, and I was invited to speak on behalf of the Arab women. Again I faced inner conflict as to whether I should take part. I did not want to go, deep down. I had never been to Tel Aviv and knew nothing of the *Histadrut*. I discussed it with some friends and they said I should go, because they trusted that I would say what had to be said. Nazareth was still full of refugees. The economy was stagnant. We were enduring military government, land expropriation, denial of work permits. Was I expected to solve such insurmountable problems? No, said my friends, but our voice must be heard.

I went. I found myself with a few other Arab women, representatives from other villages and towns. They were even more helpless than me, although there was one girl originally from Jaffa who was slightly familiar with the city. I remember that my talk emphasized the fact that you could not separate the needs of women from the needs of the community. All people needed their human rights. The Arab group was asked to meet Golda Meir, then Minister of Foreign Affairs, and I was chosen to speak on our behalf. There were two journalists present, one by the name of Tawfiq Shamoush, editor of a right-wing Jewish paper published in Arabic. The other was a woman called Shulamit.

Golda Meir reminded me of Miss Ridler, my old head-mistress. She had a stern face and she looked right through you with unflinching eyes and a determined look. I spoke in Arabic about human rights and the situation in Nazareth. I ended by saying, 'Do not make us refugees in our own country.' Tawfiq Shamoush was translating into Hebrew and what he said was, 'Do not make us refugees in your country.' Shulamit interrupted. I knew roughly what they were arguing about, because although I did not know Hebrew, the similarity between the two Semitic languages was enough to make me aware of what was going on. Golda Meir replied, 'I appreciate the speaker's courage, but our economic situation does not permit . . .' and so on and so forth. Shulamit later explained to me exactly what the interpreter had said and I thanked her for her integrity.

As I approached Nazareth on my way back from Tel Aviv, I saw a peasant in a nearby field, lying under the shade of a tree, his donkey tethered beside him. It was a peaceful, familiar reminder of the past. I clung to the memory of the scene, thinking sadly how unrelated it was to the real world of lethal weapons and political ambitions.

8
Harsh Times

It was on 19 March 1948 that Rafiq Farah, a young priest newly ordained in St Philip's Church, Nablus, was transferred by the Arab Church Council from Nablus to Haifa. The situation in Haifa was a chaotic, dangerous one, even for clergy, and many people were fleeing from the war there. As Rafiq was single and young, without family ties, he was chosen for the job of vicar and told to leave Nablus as soon as possible. He could have refused to go, but he took the last train for Haifa when many were taking the opposite direction. When he arrived, he could not leave the shelter of the railway station because of the heavy exchange of gunfire between the Jewish and Arab quarters. After two hours, the shooting subsided and he was able to take a taxi to his new home, a flat in the St Luke's Church compound.

A large number of families had already left their Haifa homes to seek refuge in Lebanon, fleeing in the general panic after the Deir Yaseen massacre. In a few weeks in April, the Jewish forces were able to occupy all areas of Haifa and then impose military rule. All the Arabs who stayed in the city were ordered to live in two areas – Abbas and the slum neighbourhood of Wadi e-Nisnas. Before the city fell, the District Commissioner asked Rafiq with two other people to be a committee responsible for the food stores in the government warehouses and for social work among the refugees. Along with the two other committee members, Rafiq ended up distributing loaves of bread and tins of sardines to the hundreds of Arabs taking refuge in churches and monasteries.

After the fall of Haifa it was dangerous work – on one occasion a sniper's bullet passed just one centimetre from his right ear. On another occasion, he was visiting a family in his clerical robes when two Jews, belonging to a terrorist group, burst in and pointed pistols to his head, accusing him of being a spy. Fortunately, one of the family members could speak Hebrew and convinced the intruders that Rafiq was their vicar, come to hold a prayer meeting at their house.

I was introduced to Rafiq by Mr Sami Geraisy, a social worker among the Arabs who was one of the other two members of the refugee committee. When Sami mentioned him, I said that my career was the most important thing and that I certainly did not want to marry a clergyman. 'But,' said Sami, 'he is more than a churchman. He is a thinker, a philosopher, so dedicated to his work that when he is out distributing rations, he often goes to bed without supper.' The last comment should have put me off – but I met Rafiq twice and was impressed. I came to admire his determination and wanted to spend all my time with him. We got married on Ascension Day, 18 May 1950, in St John's Church in Haifa.

I thought Jerusalem – my spiritual home – would be the highlight of our honeymoon but I could not believe how much it had changed. I wanted to believe that everything would be back to normal as soon as the war was over. We stayed at the YMCA, formerly a centre of cultural, social and sporting activities for Arab Christians and Muslims alike. Now it was so changed. Of course I wanted to go to my uncle's old house. As I walked along the narrow asphalt road down the hill to the house, I was trembling inside. It had been turned into a carpenter's workshop. The pepper tree was gone, there was no beautiful smell of earth from the garden. I could not enter.

Tears were rolling down my cheeks as we walked on down-hill, past the house where some Syriac friends, the Hazou family, used to live, past the headquarters of the PBS where I should have been employed and where more of my friends had worked, although they were all now scattered. At the end of the street we came to St Paul's Church where my uncle Elias preached for at least twenty years and where a thriving, good and generous community had worshipped and loved their church, and where my cousin had played the organ, and where beautiful girls came to be courted after the services by young and handsome men, before they all went to the vicarage to have coffee with my uncle's family. Now the churchyard stood empty, neglected. I went in and there was the stone tablet in memory of my uncle. Grass had grown up round it until it was scarcely visible. It seemed as if a thousand years had passed since anybody had set foot there.

We went back to the YMCA. In the lobby I caught sight of a man I knew, clearly in deep distress. His name was Ibrahim Baidas, son of the well-known writer, translator and pioneer journalist Khalil Baidas. I had got to know him and his wife Najla Mu'mmar when they fled to Nazareth from the fighting. Ibrahim had just been allowed to return to his Jerusalem house for the first time, after being granted a permit, and was devastated to find that his father's entire collection of books had been stolen. He told me how much those books meant to his father, how they could never be replaced, and he wept.

We stayed a few days in Jerusalem and I found some consolation in visiting the few Arab families that had stayed – the Sabas, the Ittayims, the Krekorians, the 'Anfouses and the dentist Dr Ibrahim George. They entertained us and a touch of the old Jerusalem was still there in their homes and lifestyle. Rafiq discussed church matters with Mr Wadie' Ittayim who thought that Jerusalem would in the end be internationalized. This was the opinion of some who argued that the Christians in Europe had sent waves of Crusaders to 'save' Jerusalem, they had then invested so much in Christian institutions in the nineteenth century, that they would never allow the city to lose its Christian presence altogether.

We returned to Haifa, a Haifa stripped of its Palestinian inhabitants and character, except for a remnant minority, under military rule and huddled mostly in the slum area of Wadi e-Nisnas. The church had been recently built to house around 700 worshippers but the congregation had dwindled to 120, the majority of whom were elderly and frail. The Anglican schools for both boys and girls had been turned into Jewish schools. The houses and beaches of some of the wealthy Arabs had become Jewish. The square of the 'horse-carriages' (Victorian light carriages, designed for two passengers), where I had once taken rides with my father, and the market adjacent to it, that had rung with the clanging of bells and the vendors' voices hawking their goods, had been demolished, along with the mosque.

I walked the streets of Haifa, passing the house where I had lived for a time with my cousin George Sima'an and his family. The houses on either side of the street had been inhabited by friends and members of the church and were now occupied by immigrants from many different countries. I stood facing my cousin's house, hearing laughter and different languages from inside. I looked at the verandas, the windows that used to look so bright with fine curtains and potted flowers. I remembered the former residents sitting on their balconies sipping Arabic coffee, in the evening as I came home from school, and the beautiful girls in their lovely dresses, their lovely hands pushing their dark hair away from their faces. I remembered a poem by that flamboyant 'Abbasid poet Abu Nawwas, better known for his poems about wine-drinking:

> House! What have the days done to you?
> They scathed you. But days can't be scathed.
> Hard times have inflicted oppression on those
> I knew to have lived in you. But times can be harsh.

I stood by the house of my cousin's family, thinking how they had been driven away from the city, losing the property they owned. According to those newly in power, it was enemy property.

I hoped to find some comfort in a prayer meeting, a Christian fellowship run by Norwegian missionaries who had been working among the Jews in Romania. We sat in a circle and the group began to pray individually, some in languages I could not understand. Those prayers which I understood were thanking God for fulfilling his promise and ingathering the Jews to their homeland and supporting them. Rafiq and I sat there, two people most definitely not included in this promise. I thought of the streets I had seen, where my friends and relatives had been driven out, and thought of their misery. They were also godly people.

Eventually we stopped going to the meetings, although the Norwegians who organized the meetings were kindly people who always cared for us and the surrounding Arab community. The questions were still bothering me, however. Was driving the Palestinians from their homeland an act of God? Was it God's will to disinherit them, some in just one night or one hour, turning them into refugees in caves and camps, homeless, lost, condemned and dispossessed? How could Christians believe this? Was this really the will of God? That a whole people should be thrown out, subjected to such suffering? How could Christians believe that God, Creator of heaven and earth, Father of Jesus Christ who became incarnate for us human beings and for our salvation, would thus treat the very creation he came to redeem? To throw out a people which he created to bring in others whom he favoured above all? I found myself immersed in the difficult, even impossible, situation of the Arab community remaining in what was called (by the Arabs) the occupied land of Palestine. The problems were immense: getting identity cards and travel permits, the attempts to reunite families, the need for education, the villagers thrown off their land within Israeli boundaries and forced to become refugees . . . Here was a people unwanted by those who had taken over authority in the land, but also refused entry into neighbouring Arab countries. At the same time, the new Law of Return gave any Jew anywhere in the world the right to come and live in Israel.

To whom could the Palestinians turn? They were truly like sheep without a shepherd. The intelligentsia, the traditional leaders and a great number of the people had either fled the war or been thrown out. It was a strange situation, worse even than being colonized, because colonizers would not usually turn you out of your own country. The few people who had any sort of talent for leadership were very much needed by those who remained. People like my husband (being a priest) were constantly sought after to act as lawyers, defenders, speakers, and channels for any governmental or non-governmental body both inside and outside Israel.

Our church work was very demanding. It felt like an emergency clinic. Most of the congregation of the church in Haifa were old and poor, jobless and displaced. Many had no houses and their children had left the country. The other congregations that came under Rafiq's direct responsibility were even worse off, like the communities in Acre and Kafr Yaseef. The churches had no organists, no choirs, no Sunday School teachers.

One of the first tasks which Rafiq undertook was to reopen St John's church school which had closed in 1948. The need for a church school was great, as it provided parents and children with a safeguard for their identity, their culture and their moral standards. The government schools for the Arabs had a programme whose chief aim was to reorientate boys and girls to the policies of Israel and to Israeli culture. The standard was lower than in the private schools and so as the students grew up, it became extremely difficult for them to find places at the Israeli universities. Those who wanted to do scientific studies – atomic physics or electronics – were refused admission. While Palestinians living in Israel constituted 15 per cent of the population, they represented only 3.5 per cent of the university population.

St John's School started with fifteen boys and girls and our first headteacher was a middle-aged lady, Mrs Zareefeh, a sweet, energetic woman whose son was one of the managers in the IPC. Numbers in the school increased so quickly that by 1959 a new building was erected to house them and when we left Haifa in 1965, there were 350 pupils. The teaching was in Arabic as the first language, followed by English and Hebrew, and the general atmosphere and standard was as the private and church schools had been in Mandate times. The school became one of the prominent institutions for Arabs in Haifa. The Catholics had managed to keep their convents and schools, which were a blessing for Arab students, and the Orthodox community also started a secondary school that filled a great gap (and is now one of the main institutions for secondary education for Arabs in Israel).

Awareness was now growing of the plight of the Palestinians and the International Christian Committee in Israel (ICCI) was set up as the channel for financial support for the impoverished Arab community, with priority given to international training and scholarship loans for secondary and university students. It also provided subsidies for Arab Evangelical schools in Haifa, Nazareth and Shefa 'Amr until 1957. The committee was appointed by the then Near East Christian Council (now Middle East Council of Churches), and Rafiq was one of the founder members. The other urgent need was to revive our national church magazine. It was first published in 1925 under the name of *al-Akbar al-Kanasiyah* (Church News).The Arab Church Council appointed my late uncle Canon Elias Marmura to be its editor; he held the job for fifteen years and was commended for his work. After 1948 the magazine continued to be issued from Jerusalem to the West Bank, Jordan and Lebanon but not to Israel.

To publish a magazine in Israel, Rafiq felt it should meet the needs of the Arab community from a Christian perspective. The name was changed to *Ar-Raied* (Pioneer) and in a limited way – being a monthly publication – it became a true mirror of the conditions and problems of the Arabs. It was also an area of our work in which I could play a substantial part, sometimes acting as editor, especially when Rafiq was away, as well as compiling the literary section. The editorial, written by Rafiq, usually dealt with the current events in Israel from the Arab perspective. It had a section for news from the Christian world, and an analytical political commentary which was usually written by a friend of ours, the late Mr Bolus Farah (no relation). He was a former Communist who had left the party when the USSR voted for the partition of Palestine, and had a long history of involvement in the defence of the rights of Arab workers during the Mandate period. When we got to know him, through his little daughter who was at St John's School, we were impressed by his sharp mind and his systematic thinking. He published three books – *Social History of the Arabs, From the Ottomans to the Hebrew State*, and *The Arab Palestinian Labour Movement* .

In Haifa I felt the need for a YWCA even more than in Nazareth, as a way of bringing together the Christians who were now a scattered minority. I corresponded with the Geneva headquarters again and established a local branch which became very successful, growing to eighty members and meeting in St Luke's Club for bazaars, lectures, parties, singing, picnics and sightseeing trips. We also had a drama group which performed scenes from the Passion story at Eastertime. Along with our Palestinian community we had Greeks, Norwegians and Armenians, as well as Muslim friends whom we invited to our functions.

And so the wheel of time was turning, to be filled with another phase of life, not only of writing, social service and activities, but also of motherhood.

9
New
Lives

In February 1951, my eldest son Amin was born. He was a
lovely baby and I could hardly believe he was mine. I was in
Nazareth, staying with my mother and under the care of the
EMMS Hospital where my friends were – Dr Doris Wilson, Dr
William Bathgate and the nurses who included Leila, Rafiq's
cousin. When our son was born Rafiq was away taking services
in Haifa, Kafr Yaseef and Shefa 'Amr. There was no public
transport and he had no car, so he had to rely on what he could
find. At times he was stopped and questioned by the military
police. He did not hear of Amin's birth until two days afterwards, through his family, and then he finally managed to
come and see us in the hospital.

While I was still in hospital, we got a letter from my brother
'Irfan who had now graduated from St John's College, Oxford.
We were looking forward to his return, if not to Israel then to
one of the Arab countries, but he wrote to say that he had been
awarded a fellowship at Princeton University in America. We
were in a way disappointed, because our desire to see him
come back and settle down outweighed our thrill at his success. It was not until nearly a year later that he was able to visit
us in Haifa. After spending a month with us, enjoying many
visitors, playing with one-year-old Amin, he left to go to
Princetown. In the course of time, I came to realize that my
brother's life was dedicated to his work of teaching and
research, especially after he took up an appointment at
Georgetown University, when he embarked on an exhaustive,
scholarly account of the seven centuries when Arab Christianity dominated the Middle East, before the arrival of Islam.
Eventually he even decided to change his surname from
Kawar to *Shahid* ('witness'), as a symbol of his work.

The Church under Threat

Also in 1951, we were faced with a very serious situation. Mr Nicola Saba, the first lay head of the Arab Church Council, was caught up in the Israeli plan of transfer of Arabs in Israel to places like Libya, Argentina and the al Jazira region in Syria – a plan studied and set by Yusif Weitz to get rid of the Arabs who remained in Israel after the 1948 Arab–Israeli war. Mr Saba was an old man and probably despairing after witnessing the mass exodus of Arabs from their country. He approached members of the Church Council to accept the transfer of the whole Arab Anglican Community to Brazil, leaving behind private and church property, and accept compensation in land and money in Brazil. Rafiq and others vehemently opposed the scheme which was born out of despair. He called for a meeting in our house and I remember him saying things like, 'We will have ample land. We will take our own carpenters, cobblers, architects, teachers' and so on and so forth.

Rafiq pointed out that we could not simply abandon our church property. It was not ours alone but was also the church for the Palestinian community worldwide, many of whom had contributed generously to its upkeep. Mr Saba dismissed the problem as trivial and easily solved. When I asked him whether he would be coming with us, he dismissed the idea as insulting. He would be going to England, together with his British wife. We told him then that we did not like the scheme and we vowed to stay and look after the church. If anybody wanted to leave, it would be their personal choice and they would pay for it out of their own pockets. After he had gone, Rafiq asked why I was laughing. I quoted the Arab proverb: 'The worst of calamities make you laugh.' I had a vision of a segregated Palestinian community somewhere in Latin America, rejected by the rest of the Palestinian people for not being faithful to what had been entrusted to their care.

The issue took a serious turn in St Luke's Club, where the Church Council held its meetings; there was much heated argument, anger and shouting. I remember sitting at home on a very warm day, apprehensive, aware that it would be even warmer in the clubhouse which was built of corrugated iron. Then two church members came in, holding up Rafiq between them. He was sweating, pale, exhausted because of the wrangling in the meeting. Rafiq and the church members were refusing to give up their responsibilities and needed all their strength to fight the proposal. The matter still did not end there. The Church Council became bitterly divided and it took a long time for the transfer proposal to be dropped and for reconciliation to take place. It was a sorry episode in the history of the Council in Israel, but, thank God, through the faithfulness and watchfulness of a few people, our church community was spared. Rafiq was then elected as Chairman of the Council after the resignation of Mr Saba, who eventually left the country.

Transfiguration

On 6 August 1952, the Feast of the Transfiguration, our second son Nabil was born. I was due to be delivered in the Nazareth hospital again, but there was no time to get there. The birth took place in my own home in Haifa, on my own bed, helped by a local midwife who was a friend from our church. I found it easy and natural, and was relieved to get the trauma of the birth over so quickly – something which I always dreaded.

At that time of year in my country, it is still hot but little fleecy clouds begin appearing in the sky and in the evening fresh breezes rustle the trees. The proverb goes: 'Transfiguration Feast says to Summer "Go away"'. Nabil's birthday has always been linked with my memories of the Feast of the Transfiguration and Mount Tabor, visible from my home town among the range of mountains, where my townspeople would pitch tents, forget the drudgery of daily life, and long to stay there, just as Christ's disciples did. The thought of it all has always given me a blissful sense of relaxation, mingled with memories of the peaceful joy usually experienced after the birth of a child.

In 1952, I had my first book of short stories published in Beirut. An English clergyman came from Jordan via the Mandelbaum Gate to visit us – we always welcomed such contacts from the outside world. He handed me a packet. Opening it, I was overwhelmed with joy. It was a copy of my book of stories, in print at last, with the title of '*Abru es-Sabil (Passers-by)*. My next concern was to see whether I could bring copies of my book into Israel, because of it having been published in the Arab world. I presented a copy to the Minister of Education and was given permission to import it, on condition that I cut out the introduction, written by my friend 'Isa Na'ouri who had overseen the publishing process. The reason given was that the text contained the phrase *nakbat Falastin* (the calamity of Palestine). I was able to order in 500 copies – the first literary books to cross the border. Some time later, I was pleasantly surprised to read a review of it in the *Jerusalem Post* by an Israeli critic who described my work as 'realistic-naturalistic yarns . . . woven out of the warp and woof that make up the human (here partly Arab) comedy, with all its hopes and fears, its grandeur and meanness, its quiet struggles and modest achievements'.

As I was living in such unhappy times, certain events and impressions would provide a spark or nucleus for some of my stories. I remember the 1959 elections, when the different Jewish parties tried to woo the remaining Arabs. Most Arab villages were in a pathetic state at that time, their only link to the world outside Israel being the radio. Newly-laid water-pipes would pass them by, going straight to the nearby kibbutz with its electricity, gardens and public services. The election situation inspired me to write a novella: *My Grandmother Goes to the Polls*. I showed the village feuds between extended families, the internal family divisions caused by allegiance to different parties, some in Israel and some in the wider Arab world. The grandmother's vote is the trump-card fought over by members of her family, each trying to tell her which way to cast it.

Another story, 'The Forsaken Olive Trees', was about a man in conflict with himself. He did not want to leave his olive grove in his village, yet his four children were sent across the border to Lebanon to escape the war. Years were passing by and he had no hope of ever seeing them again, unless he left his village for good. After my first story collection was published, I produced a slim volume of further stories entitled *Paths and Lanterns* in 1956. I wrote about a girl who lost her family after the demolition of her village, Mjeidil, which had once been a prosperous settlement. The Israelis destroyed it all, except for the convent.

Our Growing Family

The birth – also in Haifa – of my daughter, Randa, was greeted with great celebrations as I already had the two boys, Amin and Nabil. We wanted a girl to dress up in pretty frocks and hair-ribbons. Randa was and still is beautiful, with her black hair, finely-cut features and dark brown eyes. Her nickname as a little girl was the Queen of Sheba because she knew what she wanted from a very early age. On her birthday, she would never wait for her friends to come to her party but would go to call for them herself. Her friends always meant so much to her and she would go a long way to help them in any way she could. One Easter when Randa was about six years old, I took her to buy a pair of shoes. I wanted to see her in black patent leather shoes, with crossed straps like ballet slippers. She refused. She wanted the shoes with a little bow on the front. I tried to persuade her while the shopkeeper stood watching. Then he said, 'Do not try. She will always be like this.' O wise man. You knew in a second what took me a lifetime to learn!

My youngest child, my second daughter, is Karma. I still remember how from the moment she was born, she was like a little flower, her eyes a greenish-gold colour, changing according to the colour of her dress. She had fair hair and golden skin and was a sweet, gentle girl, impressionable and sensitive, shy and very attached to us, with a deep perception of people and decisive in crucial matters. At the age of three, Karma came with me to the airport when my mother went on a trip to Italy at my brother's invitation. He wanted to show her the many beautiful and historic sights, especially the ones which she had first told him about, long ago. I was worried at the prospect – my mother never travelled alone, had never been on an aeroplane, and suffered from very high blood pressure and heart problems. She was not worried, though, saying calmly, 'He will meet me at the other end. What are you fussing about?'

We took her to Lydda airport (which later became Ben Gurion airport), just after Easter, and Karma came with us, excited at the thought that *Teita* (grandmother) was going to bring back presents. As the plane took off, Karma stamped her foot and cried, 'I want *Teita* back. She has gone to heaven.' 'No, she will come back,' I told her. 'How?' asked the three-year-old. 'In the same way she went.' It sounded like the Ascension story. Two weeks later, *Teita* came back, the same way in which she went, and Karma was there to welcome her. For a present she received one of the famous Neapolitan dolls, almost as big as herself, with fair hair, blue eyes and a cherry-coloured organza dress. We called it Aphrodite!

Our children were our greatest joy. To see them growing from one stage to another was always like a new discovery. With Amin, we tried to stick to a discipline of four-hourly feeds which did not work. With Nabil, it was feed on demand which meant we enjoyed a peaceful baby! The two boys were close in age and were – and still are – close emotionally. They attended our church school, St John's, and their friends from the Arab community often came to play. We had a playground nearby which used to be a tennis court, a magnet for all the children from families who had lost their original homes and ended up in the Haifa slums. Seeing one group of children coming after another, our two boys felt it their duty to play with each party of arrivals, making it difficult for us to call them in to do their homework.

If feast days had been the highlight of my childhood, it was the same for my children, although now it was me preparing for Christmas, buying the presents and new clothes, getting the tree and decorating it with them. At Easter the neighbours would come to help decorate the Easter cakes and the children would rush about, trying to help. Getting hold of the ingredients was hard, though, because rationing was strict and no imports were allowed. However much we kept up the traditions, we could never forget the political situation which burdened our hearts. I took Nabil to buy the traditional navy-blue corduroy trousers and white shirt for Easter. He refused them. The saleswoman tried to convince him how lovely they looked, how well they matched. He still refused. He wanted jeans, wanting to move with the times, the latest fashion. It was then I realized that I belonged to the ancient regime, the old ways of doing things!

Our Haifa home was a first-floor flat which became the vicarage of our church, St John's. In the upper flat lived the Vicar of St Luke's, the church for the English-speaking ex-patriate community. In the fifteen years that we lived there, the occupants of the upper flat changed more than once but we had good relations and shared Chritian fellowship with all of them. In our first two years there, Rafiq's three brothers stayed with us, being unable to return to their village home because of the difficulty of obtaining permits. My mother was also living with us by then and was a great help to me, as well as being our church organist. She was often sick, however, suffering from high blood pressure and heart problems. I had occasional home help, but it was often not available when I needed it most.

In the Middle East, a vicar's home is called *Beit al-Umma* ('the house of the nation') meaning that it does not belong to the family alone, and that anybody can come at any time. If the vicar is not at home, it is the duty of the wife to welcome the visitors and sit with them. We welcomed people wholeheartedly, especially those coming from outside Haifa. Young men and women liked to come to talk politics, literature and religion. Friends came too, especially from Nazareth, and Rafiq's relatives from his village. We also had gatherings of thinking people – lawyers, poets, teachers – to discuss the latest political situation, the latest military operations. Whatever else happened, it was the national calamity which consumed our time, attention and emotions.

No one day was like another. Visitors would often turn up as early as six in the morning. Our living-room was in the middle of the house and visitors would be in a strategic position to see members of the family as they walked about or went to the kitchen. Rafiq always took his time to get ready and so even though I might have had a sleepless night with my children, I had to go and sit with the callers. It is disrespectful in the Middle East to leave them waiting by themselves, especially if they have come from another village or town. This meant it must be an urgent matter as they would have had to go to so much trouble to get a travel permit, standing and queuing for hours.

Social problems were acute. Old people who were left behind when the younger generation left, sometimes voluntarily, sometimes compulsorily, needed much care. Their problems usually stemmed from housing. Israelis had either occupied their houses or – if they shared them – the newcomers would use any means to throw the old people out. One old woman, who no longer had any family in Israel, lived in a room with a balcony while her neighbours occupied the other rooms in the house. They used strange, brutal ways to make her leave, such as dressing up as ghosts to frighten her. She would come and stay for hours with us, bringing with her the parts from her Primus stove for fear that the neighbours might steal it, to make things more difficult for her.

The Mandelbaum Gate

At Christmas Israel allowed a certain number of Christians to cross to the Arab side of Jerusalem, to the Old City to visit the holy places. They were allowed to go for thirty-six hours only and had to cross through the Mandelbaum Gate (named after a house that belonged to a Jewish family). The names of all those going had to be checked and accepted by both the Israelis and the Jordanians. Applications were ready from September and the names were submitted to the government officials. Rafiq was distressed when the authorities asked the clergy to put forward a certain number of applicants because people then believed that their names would be accepted at once, on account of the clerical recommendation. The chance to visit was not so much to see the holy places as to meet with family members from whom they had been separated for so long, especially members of the immediate family – a mother whose children were across the border, or families who would come from new homes in Syria, Iraq, Egypt, Lebanon or the Gulf to visit an old father. Mandelbaum Gate became known as the Gate of Tears.

Cars started arriving there in the small hours of the morning, but however early we went, we found crowds already there before us. Some would have come a whole day beforehand. Crossing the border was expensive. The 1950s were very harsh years economically and Ben Gurion was always emphasizing the need for tightening belts. Coupons were used to mark how much you could buy and you spent much time doing calculations and weighing up your priorities. Israel did not allow the import of foreign currency and you were only allowed to take out a maximum of five pounds, even though Israeli money was not accepted outside the country. We waited in line at the Gate. Nobody felt friendly towards the other bystanders because precious hours were slipping by. We had only thirty-six hours over the border but what if our destination was Amman or another city in Jordan? The cold was biting. Children in their new coats, looking like teddy bears in their woollen hats and gloves, soon lost their excitement and got tired and hungry, needing the toilet. We were treated harshly by the soldiers and there was an equally harsh reception on the Jordanian side. A cousin of mine, whose son was coming from Beirut to meet him, was threatened with being turned back at the Gate. It turned out that his name was similar to another who had been rejected as a suspected Communist and my cousin had to wait from 5.00 am until 2.00 pm until his name was cleared.

We never forgot the moment at the Mandelbaum Gate when the meetings took place. A father might not recognize his son at first. Then would come the realization, the embraces, the tears that summed up so many emotions. Was it sadness? Joy? We heard exclamations of despair when the one awaited did not turn up. 'His plane is late from the Gulf!' 'The flight was cancelled!' The children were the most bewildered, when introduced to relatives from the other side. 'This is Auntie Jameeleh' or 'This is *Teita*' (grandmother). 'Come, my love.' And the child would be hugged by an old woman with a wrinkled face and bony hands. Then the crowd would disperse, each to a momentary feast of being together.

Buying things was another phase in this short drama. The Palestinian coming from Israel had been missing much of what is usually in the Arab *suk* – spices, coffee, Arabic sweets, blankets, fabrics, suits and nylon stockings (for a few years Israel recycled old clothes which were harsh on the skin). The hosts were willing to indulge the newcomers from occupied lands and gladly brought them presents, but if you wanted to take gifts out of Israel, you had to remember that any item with Hebrew writing on it got the bearer into trouble.

Family members talked together, sharing their bitterness about the Palestinian situation and remembering the homes they had left, until they had to go back. The scene at the Gate of the previous day was re-enacted without the slightest ray of joy, as people huddled together, realizing the gulf between them and those who bade them farewell. The presents were a great problem. There was a thorough check of every article and duty had to be paid on them, either in scarce foreign currency or in Israeli liras which people had hidden some-where. In the days after their return, visitors came to greet the pilgrims and hear about their adventures, share their joy of being reunited with loved ones, and taste the Arabic sweets. Talking about the visit made it seem worth the heartache. After all, so much had happened and sunk into the soul. 'My son has a good job in the Gulf. He is married but his wife could not come.' 'I was sorry for my neighbour – her daughter could not come. It seems she is not happily married.' 'You should see Amman (or Ramallah). Such beautiful buildings.'

Mandelbaum Gate was a symbol of a divided soul, of separa-tion from a world, a culture, where we belonged. As for myself, I felt so estranged on coming back that I could hardly bear to start life again. My heart was stolen from me and everything around me seemed desolate as I watched the State of Israel being built on the suffering bodies of my people.

10

Haifa and Beyond

There were many political changes during the 1950s and 1960s, especially in what were known as Third World countries. I cannot describe my early years of married life, with all its church and social commitments, without mentioning the effect of those changes, especially in the Arab world and for those of us who stayed within the boundaries of Israel.

Amid all the frustrations and humiliations inflicted by the harsh military rule, most of us were like prisoners in a cell with just one window through which to see the outside world. This window was the transistor radio which made us feel that we still belonged to the wider Arab world. Its events and struggles, its hopes and concerns, its disillusionment or success were ours too. One special station fed our insatiable appetite: *Sawt el-'Arab* (Voice of the Arabs). Its rhetoric aroused the feelings of the masses and stirred the liberation movements in many countries in Asia and Africa. Our young poets became the mouthpieces of such sentiments. When we heard of the rise of the movement of the Free Officers in Egypt, the demise of the old regime ending with the expulsion of King Farouk in a bloodless coup d'état, and the rise of 'Abdal Nāsir, it was like the breath of life to a dying person. The Arab world was well aware of the extent of the corruption that had dug deep into the country. Soon Palestinian listeners were declaring, 'This is not a coup but a revolution!' The poverty of the Egyptian peasants was well known and Nasser was bringing in an Arab socialism that developed internally, rather than a political system imported from elsewhere.

Who knows what judgement history will finally pass on Nasser? To the majority of Arabs who remained in Israel he was sent by God. Our ears were glued to the radio when President Nasser of Egypt spoke. Shops were closed and people rushed to their homes and congregated round that magical apparatus to listen to him. His charisma seemed to reach us through the airwaves. In 1955, speaking in Alexandria, he addressed the crowds in his resonant voice, 'The Suez canal is ours – 120,000 Egyptians dug it with their blood and sweat.' He told them that he had decided to nationalize the canal and the crowds cheered. Also that year he attended the Afro-Asian conference in Indonesia, with Nehru of India, Chou En-lai of China and Sokarno of Indonesia, where they declared their intention of creating a neutral power bloc, 'neither East nor West'. Was this not what we had always wanted? Ever since Turkish times, since the dawn of history, our Arab world had been subject to the whim and wills of others, and in modern times subject to the greed and snobbery of the Western world. We listened to Nasser on our radio, elated. We had a leader now. He had captured the imagination of the Arab world but for us Palestinians, he embodied hope. We looked with pride at Cairo. Nasser had made it a centre of power for Third World countries, where leaders who had achieved the liberation of their own countries would confer with him. The broadcasters sang his praises.

If our hearts and minds were following Nasser's speeches, we were brought back to our own miserable situation on 29 October 1956, when a curfew was imposed and we were ordered to black out our windows. It was the outbreak of the Suez War, precipitated by Nasser's assertion of control over the canal, in defiance of Anthony Eden, the British Prime Minister. I remember what an awful night that was, how I feared for my children, as we scotchtaped black cloth on the windows and the glass doors. I was not only afraid of the war, but suddenly felt that we were in the enemy camp. The next day, the streets were empty. We sat in suspense and fear while in the south Israel invaded Sinai. Then came the ultimatum issued by France and Britain, calling on Egypt and Israel to cease fighting and withdraw their forces ten miles from the canal.

Israel accepted the ultimatum – the country would lose nothing, because its forces were nowhere near the canal at the time so that a ten mile withdrawal would still entail a massive advance from the pre-conflict boundaries. Nasser who, by the terms of the ultimatum, would have had to abandon territory he had not yet lost, rejected it. The Anglo-French forces assembled in Cyprus and landed near Port Said. We stayed at home, tense and angry at the invasion of Port Said, talking, arguing, listening, waiting. The local people stood up to the foreign armies with great courage, blocking the canal with scores of ships, while the Syrians had blown up the pipe-lines and pumping stations on their territory. It looked as if it would be an Arab victory.

Two days later, some friends came to our house, bringing stories of a massacre in Kafr Qasim, an Arab village in Israel. One man said, 'Come on, don't spread rumours of this sort. It's too much. They would never do such a thing' but he was mistaken. It had happened like this. On 29 October, the day the curfew was imposed, an army officer called on the *mukhtar* (head of the village) of Kafr Qasim at 4.30 pm, giving him the order for the curfew to start at 6.00 pm that evening. The *mukhtar* replied, 'But there are 400 people already outside the village. I don't have enough time to call them all back.' The officer promised that everyone returning from work would be allowed to pass safely, on his authority and on that of the Israeli Government. At 5.00 pm the massacre started at the west end of the village. Forty-seven people were killed, among them women and children. Two members of the *Knesset* (Israeli Parliament), Tawfiq Toubi (an Arab) and Meir Vilner (a Jew), were able to get to the village, although it was under seige, and passed on the story of what had happened to a journalist. The case was brought to the *Knesset* by Tawfiq Toubi but all that resulted was a three-year prison sentence for one man, who was later pardoned. The officer who gave the order was merely reprimanded and given a token fine of one penny.

We heaved a sigh of relief when the PLO, the Palestine Liberation Movement, emerged. Read backwards, the initials of its Arabic name spelt *Fatah* (Victory). We rejoiced that the title included the word 'Palestine' because the very name of our country was seldom heard. The kingdom of Jordan, which had annexed part of Palestine, called it the West Bank. According to a speech by Golda Meir, Palestinians no longer existed and never did. We were to be considered refugees, not people with an identity and a country. Now, with the founding of the PLO, the name of our country could warm our hearts and bring hope with it. Years later, when I lived in Beirut, I noticed that the PLO was the physical embodiment of Palestine, especially to those in the camps. To me in Israel it certainly became so.

Having said that the existence of a Palestine organization gave me a ray of hope, I was never in favour of the attacks of the *fedayeen* (freedom fighters) on Israel. What I believed – and still believe – is that the greatest power lay in Arab unity. I also saw that the *fedayeen* attacks would give Israel the excuse to retaliate, usually out of all proportion to the harm done. We ended up being stigmatized as terrorists, when we were the victims of one of the greatest onslaughts on one people's history and civilization. There were many, however, who believed that fighting was the only way to awaken the world to our plight. It was the only means the PLO had. On its own, the organization could not influence the Arab world to unite and take non-violent measures against Israel and its allies. What seemed to the world like sudden violent resistance was the outcome of long anguish in the soul of the Palestinians in Israel and elsewhere.

Arabic Culture in Exile

Poetry has always been the medium used by Arabs to express themselves. From pre-Islamic times it has been a power behind every movement. A group of young poets was now emerging who surprised us with their spontaneity, their new poetic diction, modernism and courage. They spoke from bitter experience, many of them having been arrested and placed in administrative detention. I knew many of them personally, as they either came to visit us or contributed to *Ar-Raied*, our magazine. Although these poets were cut off from the mainstream of Arabic culture, and some of them barely given any secondary education, they presented a poetry which rejected the onslaught on their human rights, confident yet asking again and again why they and their people should be deprived of both country and identity. Throughout the Arab world, they were acclaimed as the Poets of the Resistance.

On 30 July 1957, I attended a meeting in the club *Ikha* ('Brotherhood') to form the Arab Writers' Union. Its aims were to preserve and promote Arabic culture, to upgrade standards of Arabic teaching, encourage Arabic publishing, carry on with research and translation, and defend freedom of thought and personal expression. A rally to launch the union was planned in the Cinema Empire in Nazareth (since it was the largest Arab city) and I was chosen to be a speaker, along with some of the Poets of the Resistance, taking the subject of 'Literature reflects Arab Nationalism and has accompanied its path since the Arab Renaissance'. The cinema was full and the speeches had to be broadcast through loudspeakers to the hundreds of people standing outside. Some sat in their cars, some gathered in nearby shops and many simply stood in the middle of the street. It was like a big demonstration with some people clapping and cheering, some leaning from the balconies to watch. It was as if we had temporarily forgotten Israeli rule and its iron hand. Next day, all the speakers had to give an account of their contribution to their respective employers. Some working in education lost their jobs as a result. I was simply reprimanded.

My own writing continued, meanwhile. I had a collection of poetic prose pieces published in 1959, called *Scents and Echoes*. Also in 1959 I wrote a play based on the story of Shahrazad and the *Thousand and One Nights*, while in 1961 my dramatic scenes on the Life and Passion of Jesus were published in a book called *The King of Glory*. They proved to be helpful for schools and Christian institutions. In 1963, I produced a further collection of short stories, *To Whom Is The Spring*. One story had the rather exotic title of 'The Call of Damascus and the Rebuke of the Pomegranates'. It told of the longings of those Arabs living in Israel and separated from the rest of their people, and those living outside their country, separated from home and land. It used the story of a boy in a refugee camp who always dreamt that he was called to go back and pick the ripening pomegranates in his lost home village.

A Taste of England

In 1960 Rafiq was chosen to go on a one-year diploma course at St Augustine's Central College of the Anglican Communion in Canterbury, England. This college was started by the Anglican Communion to bring together Anglican clergy from different parts of the world, who had heavy responsibilities and stressful jobs. Having previously visited England in 1955 for the YWCA centenary celebrations, I was delighted to be able to join Rafiq for the last term and found it a great privilege to hear the lectures. I enjoyed the fellowship and made many friends, meeting clergy and their wives from all over the world, especially Africa and Asia. I also found it exciting to attend services in the great cathedral. The experience helped me to see the diversity and historical roots of the church. Sadly, the college closed in 1967 due to lack of funds. It was much needed to refresh, instruct and encourage people like us who faced difficulties in our home countries and could so easily feel ignored and forgotten.

Ever since we were first married, Rafiq and I thought it a good idea to read something together to feed our souls. We were not always organized, and days slipped by without this spiritual nourishment, but on the whole we kept up our daily reading and meditation. This was always helpful to me, especially when I was feeling low and even doubtful – for my spiritual journey was never easy.

I cannot attribute all my religious difficulties to the fundamentalist interpretation of the Bible carried out by a sizable number of Christians, but it was certainly a cause of dismay and frustration for many Palestinian Christians. I found the link made between the Promised Land and the modern state of Israel contradictory to Jesus' teaching. He never renounced the teaching, inspiration and religious experience of the Old Testament and neither did I as his follower, but he questioned much, and so did I. The Holocaust was a shameful crime in the history of humanity. It seemed to me that the West paid for its war crimes, satisfied its pangs of conscience and received God's forgiveness for the Holocaust by giving the Jews a homeland – and thereby making the Palestinians scapegoats, carrying the sins of the world. Two wrongs did not make a right.

Death in Haifa

On the afternoon of 17 September 1961, nine-year-old Nabil came back from school saying that he had seen the naked, dead bodies of five boys on an open truck driving to Wadi e-Nisnas. He had heard women screaming. Not long after, we found out what had happened. The five boys, fed up with living in the slums and attracted by President Nasser's rhetoric, had decided to try and cross the border, to escape to what they assumed would be a land of pure happiness and

freedom. They were intercepted and shot by some Israeli soldiers on their way to Gaza. Israeli soldiers were accused of
mutilating the bodies, but Israel claimed that the Egyptians
had carried out the work. Wadi e-Nisnas echoed with the
misery and lamentation over the five dead.

Our church school stood not far from the street leading to
the slum quarter and some of the boys' relatives came to our
house, demanding an investigation into the deaths, refusing to
believe that the youths had been shot by the Egyptians. 'The
Arabs must protest, distribute leaflets', they said. 'We have so
much proof that the boys never got to the Egyptian border.'
Aba Houshi, the mayor of Haifa, ordered that the bodies
should be buried at night, but the parents of three of them
demanded a church funeral because they had been Catholic,
and asked Rafiq to attend. On 21 September crowds gathered
from Nazareth and the surrounding villages, packing the street
by midday. A long, sad procession – thousands of Arabs –
accompanied the mourners to the Greek Catholic church of
Mar Elias. Some of the mothers walked barefoot with their
hair down as a sign of mourning, crying their heartbreaking
dirges. The crowd shouted patriotic slogans.

In the church, the mothers asked that the mutilated bodies
be uncovered and that Rafiq should be one of the witnesses.
Then, when the service was over, they emerged to find themselves encircled by Israeli armoured cars. In the cemetery,
there was some hesitation as to whether the boys should be
buried together, but the crowd cried out, 'They are the sons of
the people.' The boys were laid to rest in one grave. Rafiq later
headed what became known as the 'Committee of Thirteen'
and called for a press conference to repeat the demand for a
public inquiry into the circumstances of the shooting.

Moving On

By 1965, seventeen years had elapsed since Rafiq had come to
Haifa. There had been times when he was the only Anglican
Arab priest serving all seven congregations in different parts of
Israel, as well as chairing the Church Council that controlled
the administration of the congregations. Now, with the arrival
in Israel of three other theologically trained Arab Anglican
priests, ensuring that the churches were well staffed, the time

seemed ripe for a move. We also felt that the Jerusalem diocese was still one church and that a change of priests would strengthen unity and maintain a sense of continuity. I was myself longing for a change, feeling the heaviness of living under Israeli rule and longing for a different sort of life, a life with more intellectual stimulation. We also had to think of our children, as we had no money to educate them abroad, although life in Israel was easier for the younger generation. They were not, like me, haunted by the past, not reminded of streets that used to have Arabic names, nor nostalgic about Palestine.

Our lives in Haifa were always busy, full of people and meetings and work, but deep down I felt a sense of futility. I did not belong. I remember pushing my babies in their pram and feeling a shudder run through me when I saw a street with a new Hebrew name instead of the Arabic one which I remembered. I saw the countryside changing swiftly from the Arab villages that blended with the landscape, to kibbutzim. How often did I stand at my bedroom window, looking out at the olive tree in the garden, and feeling that I wanted just to stay there with the tree, dreaming of the past? I knew I could not go on living with such sadness, such depression. Sometimes we took our children to the public gardens at Mount Carmel. As the shadow of the long pines lengthened on the ground, so did my melancholy. I would try to see Ras-e-Nakoura, the ridge that divided Lebanon from Israel, white where the sun shone on it. I would gaze and gaze, telling myself, 'My people are there. There is my soul and there is where I belong.'

We decided to ask Bishop Qubain in Jerusalem if we could move to the eastern part of the city, at that time still controlled by Jordan. In the spring of 1965, permission was finally granted. It was generally almost impossible for Arabs in Israel to be allowed into Arab countries. There were no diplomatic ties – or indeed any other kind of contact – between Israel and the Arab countries and the borders were closed except for entry to Jerusalem at Christmas, for foreign diplomats, and for a few Christian clerics from the Catholic Church who had Vatican passports. An exchange of priests was, however, considered a different matter.

It was hard to wrench ourselves from our fellow Arabs whom we had struggled to help, and from the congregations whom we had served for so long. There was sadness and disbelief as the people in the churches heard about our decision to go. We were part of their religious, political and social life. Rafiq was somebody to whom they always turned, whatever the problem – housing, work permits, identity cards, crossing at Christmas, scholarships for their children, consolation in bereavement. So, although I knew I needed a change, I could share the people's sadness and understand how they felt. For the Arab community, the departure of any family made us feel more vulnerable. I knew that others had been resilient, had stayed, but I was yearning for another life.

The practical side of leaving was no less fraught. We were limited as to what we could take and further hampered by the instruction that no Jewish-style furniture was allowed over the border or even anything bearing Hebrew script. There was no market for second-hand furniture so we had to decide what to take and what to give away. And we had so many books, so many photographs! Also, by leaving Israel we forfeited our rights to any social security or pensions, because we were considered to be moving to enemy territory. Then came the round of farewell parties. Each family from our congregation invited us, as well as many of our friends and relatives. Our friends Sami and Adele Geraisy suggested that we meet for a family outing, their way of bidding us farewell. We went to 'Ein Jalut where there was a public park with running water, and where the children – Sami and Adele had four boys, besides our two boys and two girls – could play together, as they were of a similar age.

This place was claimed by both Arab and Jew as historical, but for different reasons. The Jews remembered there the battle when Gideon defeated the Midianites. The Arabs remembered the battle of 1259 between the Egyptian Mamluk rulers and the Mongols under Genghis Khan, when the Palestinians fought valiantly with the Egyptians and stopped the ruthless invaders who had swept through the steppes of Asia, bringing havoc and destruction to cities such as Baghdad and Damascus. On our farewell visit to the park, we stayed until evening. As we were thinking of leaving, an American youth appeared, as if from nowhere. He looked haggard, hungry, afraid. He greeted us and we invited him to share our food. He did so, saying he had not eaten for some time. A while later, he began to tell us how afraid he was of the Arabs. He had heard that they had tails, that they were cannibals. We listened to all this and then, before he left, thanking us for our kindness, we told him that we were Arabs. To say the least, he was greatly surprised.

A final farewell service took place in the church, followed by speeches in the churchyard, with all our friends and members of the church round. Nur Edin el-'Abasi, a much-respected man from the Muslim community (and an inspector at the Department of Education in Mandate times), gave one of the speeches, saying: 'We are not only bidding farewell to a vicar who is the head of a Christian community, whom we respect and with whom we have worked, but also to a man who stood by us in all situations as a defender, helper, friend and adviser. He stayed with us in dangerous times when others were leaving.' The shadows lengthened, lights shone from neighbouring houses. The school and the church seemed to stare silently at us as we left, as if hoping desperately that others would carry on the work.

On our last day, I went into each room of our house and said goodbye. I looked through my window at the olive tree and thought of the moments of peace I had found there. I knew I would remember that house all my life, the place where my children were born and where they had spent their childhood. We set off in the car, with a truck behind carrying the belongings of fifteen years of married life. Well-wishers stood at the Mandelbaum Gate for a final goodbye and we cried. Was this not after all the Gate of Tears? We crossed the border, turned, and waved one last time to our true and loving friends.

11
Through the Mandelbaum Gate

Who was there to greet us when we arrived? Nobody from the church, but only Rafiq's nephew, Munir. The children were tired and thirsty, my mother exhausted. A Jordanian truck came to take our belongings. Arriving at St George's Cathedral in East Jerusalem, we could not find the gatekeeper who had the key to our new home. Eventually somebody fetched him from his house and he gave us the key to a house in Wadi el-Joz.

When we got there, our disappointment was immense. Narrow, high steps led to two small bedrooms. The kitchen could fit only one person at a time. How could seven people live in such a small flat? We spent our first night at the house of Rafiq's sister, Salwa. Her husband and five children were always welcoming. Over the next few days, we had apologies from the church authorities. They said that everybody was away and that our moving date had been overlooked which explained why there had been nobody to welcome us at the border. We worried about the smallness of the house assigned to us. Fortunately the Archbishop was understanding and suggested that we look for another place to live. At last we managed to find somewhere in Beit Hanina, near the main road running north from Jerusalem. Many Palestinians, originally from the area, which included the old village of Beit Hanina, were returning after spending time abroad earning money, and building new houses and villas. Regular bus services connected the neighbourhood with the town of Ramallah.

Our apartment overlooked a fairly big garden which held two houses, each divided into two flats. We agreed to rent the upper flat in one of the houses, facing the paved walkway to the gate. It had an enclosed veranda with huge glass windows overlooking the garden with its plum, apple and olive trees, vines and flowerbeds, and Rafiq decided to use half of it as his study. The other half became our sitting-room.

I bought many metres of calico material and a few metres of

floral print fabric to sew curtains – plain with a floral border – and our furniture and embroidered cushions helped make the room beautiful. I had shelves put up to display our collection of Hebron glass, our brass vases and house plants. The master bedroom had a balcony with a lovely view of Mount Nebi Samuel, cornfields, olive trees. Even as I write, I recall the joy I felt at finding myself back in Arab surroundings, watching the women walking past like royalty in their embroidered Palestinian dresses, on their way to catch the local bus to Ramallah. Amin and Nabil were registered at St George's School in Jerusalem, while Randa and Karma attended the German convent school known as Schmidt Girls' School, so that all four of them were receiving just the sort of education which I had wanted for my children.

Bishop Angus Campbell MacInnes had been enthroned as Archbishop of Jerusalem in 1957. His province comprised the dioceses of Jerusalem, Iran, Egypt, Libya, Sudan, Cyprus, the Gulf and Iraq. The Arab parishes had been demanding an Arab bishop for some time and so in 1958, on the Feast of the Epiphany (6 January), Bishop Qubain was consecrated as Bishop of Jordan, Lebanon and Syria, the first Arab Anglican bishop.

Trouble loomed when Rafiq learned from Bishop Qubain that the position he was to occupy – Secretary for Christian Literature in the Near East Council of Churches – no longer existed. We had no Jordanian passport and could not leave the country to look for another post. Then Rafiq was offered two jobs: secretary for the Bible Society in Jerusalem and correspondent for the Voice of the Gospel radio station, far less demanding work than he had been doing in Haifa. The move was good for my son Nabil. The asthma from which he had long suffered nearly disappeared and he made excellent progress at school. But we were now in the 1960s. I found my apartment housing a rock band, the Silvertones, with drums, electric guitars and boys with long hair. Nabil wore his curly hair down to his shoulders, his trousers deliberately patched and tattered. The headmaster and teachers at his school expected us to make him have a haircut, but we expected the school to enforce such rules.

The band practised for a performance in the MacInnes Hall, next to the school. When the great day came, my ears were throbbing – and not with silvery tones, either. The performance was excellent, though, and all the mothers (including me) who had complained about the noise were very proud to see their boys swaying, hair flying as they played. We refused to take their music seriously, however, never for a moment believing that such a style could last.

As for me, I began writing for a daily newspaper, *Al-Jihad*. Although I was paid very little, it gave me scope to publish a serialized novella, a daily short article on current issues, a weekly essay on any subject I chose, and a column entitled *Diary of a Mother*. I joined the Cathedral guild and the local YWCA, later becoming a member of the Jerusalem Board. I also contributed to the Jordanian Hashemite broadcasting station and wrote occasionally for a literary magazine, *Afkar*, published in Amman.

The cathedral, with its close, hostel, garden and college, was a focal point in our lives. On Sundays we went to the Arabic service and many of the congregation went to the house of Bishop and Mrs Qubain for coffee afterwards, enjoying the chance to chat to friends and acquaintances. With the coffee, Mrs Qubain served soft sugary sweets shaped like pink and yellow shoes which my girls loved to eat there, although when I bought packets of them home, they seldom looked at them. I especially loved going to the hostel and looking at the garden. It was a source of joy and peace to me, even nostalgia. I loved walking along the corridor leading to the garden, decorated with Palestinian pottery, brass trays, tables with Palestinian tiles painted with birds and blossom, hanging baskets of flowers. The garden itself was a magical profusion of colour and sweet-scented blooms, roses, fuschias, marguerites, lilies, carnations, daisies, morning glory and ivy growing up the old walls, as well as an orange and an olive tree. The beauty was a testament to the talents of the warden, John Rose.

One of the gardeners working there was Yousef, trained by John Rose. When I last visited the garden in 1992, he was still there, although the garden had changed. Although Yousef was illiterate, he knew the English names of all the flowers and plants in the garden. To watch him working in such peaceful, sheltered surroundings, away from the problems and frustrations of the Palestinians in Jerusalem, was very pleasant. I almost envied him his task but then I learned from one of the other members of staff that Yousef's three sons were in prison. From then on, I used sometimes to try and imagine Yousef's thoughts as he tended the flowers blooming in the garden of St George's hostel.

Archbishop Campbell MacInnes retired in November 1969. With his going, I felt an era had passed as he spent years in Palestine and Rafiq and I had known him for many years. His father had been Bishop in Jerusalem and his mother retired there, after her husband's death, to become secretary for the Church Missionary Society in Palestine. Campbell MacInnes had been headmaster of Bishop Gobat School from 1930 to 1943, and was known to hundreds of Palestinian students, as well as Muslim Arabs and Armenians who remembered him with great love and respect. He also provided the impetus for the founding of St George's Theological College, a centre in the Holy Land for fieldwork, study and reflection. To our family, the Archbishop and his wife were always 'The Bishop and Auntie Bishop', for so Randa, then aged six, had announced them when they once came to visit us in Haifa.

Archbishop George Appleton then arrived, appointed by the Archbishop of Canterbury to plan the reorganization of the Church in the Middle East. The final result of his work was the 1976 inauguration of the Middle East province of the Anglican Church and the creation of a new Jerusalem diocese, with a Palestinian Arab diocesan bishop, Fayek Haddad, the first to be appointed since 1841. With the handover of various mission institutions, the new diocese took charge of more than thirty hospitals, schools, old people's homes, orphanages, homes for the mentally handicapped and the deaf. The diocese covered Syria, Lebanon, Israel, the West Bank and Jordan, serving and meeting the needs of people regardless of race, religion or nationality.

Many Palestinian Christians were critical of the Church's stand on the Palestinian question. For many years humanitarian aid had been extended to the Palestinians, who were classed as refugees, but there was a reluctance to take a stand on issues of justice and human rights, issues of the identity and birth rights of the Palestinian people. With the foundation of the new diocese, however, there began to be a greater focus on the experiences of the Palestinians and attempts were made to reinterpret the theology that linked the land of Palestine with the Jews. This created a liberation theology with justice as the focus, rather than the idea that God might be a partisan, tribal god, supporting only Israel. Canon Naim Ateek, a Palestinian Anglican priest, is leading a group on Palestinian liberation theology in Jerusalem.

During our time in Beit Hanina, my writing and speaking work continued. After attending a conference in Beirut, connected with the Near East Christian Council (NECC), on Christian literature, I suggested to Archbishop Appleton that we should publish a Christian magazine for the intelligentsia on the West Bank. We managed to publish two numbers of what we called *The Earth Our Ship*, but although it was a very worthwhile venture, we could get no help with distribution. I also wrote plays for the United Nations Work and Relief Agency (UN-WRA) schools in Ramallah, Bir Zeit and the Evangelical Home in Ramallah, as well as contributing to the annual Passion Play, performed in front of worshippers from all denominations who came to attend the services at both St George's Cathedral (Anglican) and the Church of the Redeemer (Lutheran).

To help with the housework, we engaged a girl from a nearby village. Naddiya was a clean and methodical worker, but I gradually started to notice how much time she spent on beautifying herself. She had two free afternoons when she was allowed out and I realized that whenever she went to the Old City, she would come back with the most expensive clothes, satin nightdresses and slips, gold slippers, costly make-up and perfumes, patterned silk scarves, chiffon shawls. Her family were very poor and Naddiya and her sister worked to help their father. When I said to her, 'What is this, Naddiya? This is extravagant', she shrugged and smiled mysteriously. When she got up to work first thing in the morning, she would wear lipstick, kohl and face-powder, her skirt was tight and short, with a broad belt emphasizing her waist – she was not dressed for everyday household duties at all. She was always on the veranda or near the windows that opened on the garden. I noticed that the landlord would also be there, the transistor radio loudly playing Arabic love songs such as 'When will you return to me, my love?' Once, while we were out, he came to our apartment, accusing my boys and their friends of picking the plums from his fruit-trees, calling for the police to arrest them. I could not understand his behaviour, when my sons refused to touch any fruit. The plums in front of the house would fall, rot and blacken the ground without anyone picking them. And when we first came to the house, he had said, 'Consider this tree as yours. Please pick the fruit when it ripens.'

It did not take me long to put the pieces of the jigsaw together. It was a way of coming to the house and seeing Naddiya. The expensive things she bought were probably purchased with money he gave her. Perhaps it was him she met in the Old City on her afternoons off. Perhaps he came to see her when we were out on Sundays. When I voiced my suspicions to my friends, they told me that she should be sent away at once. If anything serious happened, we would be held responsible because she was considered to be in our care. I thought such drama belonged on the cinema screen – how could I bring myself to tell Naddiya that she must leave?

Next morning, at six o' clock, there was a knock at the door. It was Naddiya's mother. Naddiya's youngest sister had died and they wanted her home for a few days. After saying how sorry I was, I added, 'I can't have Naddiya back. Times are bad and it's too much of a responsibility. If I need her, I'll call her back.' Naddiya was very surprised but her mother told her to go and get her things. In a very short time, they were leaving. I went out of the door to see them off and caught sight of something in a packet on the windowsill. When I unpacked it there were Naddiya's gold slippers. Did she leave them to make an excuse for coming back? Or was it as an omen, that if you leave something that belongs to you, you are bound to come back? I did not stop to ponder. I ran after her and called. Her mother turned. 'You have forgotten your slippers.' Naddiya seemed dismayed. I never saw her again.

12
God's Furnace

Since 1948, many changes had taken place in the Middle East, but none were powerful or effective enough to bring justice to the Palestinians whose situation in the refugee camps was deteriorating, their dissatisfaction mounting. Many of the liberation movements welcomed with euphoria in the 1950s and 1960s later ran into trouble. Attempts at Arab unity came to nothing, nationalists and Communists attacked each other in Iraq, while Nasser's involvement in the new Arab republic in Yemen aroused the hatred of the conservative monarchies in Saudi Arabia, drained Egypt's foreign currency and employed up to 50,000 of his troops for five years.

The difficulty that faced the Palestinian fighters was (and still is) that they could never have a base of their own. They were always dependent on their host countries. This made them not only vulnerable, but subject to internal disputes as different factions succumbed to the influence of the host nation. When their agenda clashed with that of their hosts, they were in serious trouble, having to fight on two fronts. And, as always, Israeli reprisal attacks were out of all proportion to the Palestinian attack which was used as a pretext for a policy of annihilation. This in turn upset the host country which saw its civilians killed, villages destroyed and land occupied, as was the case in Lebanon.

In April 1967, there were clashes between Israel and Syria, the former warning that reprisals would be serious if commandos continued to carry out sabotage in Israel. Nasser was warned by Syrian, Soviet and Egyptian intelligence that Israel would attack Syria. Then three Israeli soldiers were killed by a mine explosion near the Jordanian frontier, near the small West Bank village of Samou' in the Hebron hills. The West Bank population, whose resentment and frustration had been building over the years, rose up in protest, expecting Israeli retaliation and demonstrating against the inadequate protection offered by the Jordanian army. Meanwhile, the towns of Ramallah, Nablus, Jenin and the Old City of Jerusalem were in revolt. Nasser was taunted with the fact that his Sinai borders were still under the UN Emergency Force. Why had he not retaliated after the Israeli diversion of the river Jordan? Why not close the Straits of Tiran to Israeli ships, if the Egyptian army was as strong as it claimed to be?

On Monday 5 June 1967, the June War broke out. Amin was in Jerusalem at school, sitting his exams. Rafiq had taken me by car to a little hospital in Beit Hanina for a check-up. While I had my appointment, Rafiq sat in the car, listening to the radio. Suddenly he came running in to where I was sitting with the doctor. 'War has been declared. The Israelis are bombing from the air.' We were terrified. 'I must go to Jerusalem and get Amin back,' Rafiq went on. I hurried home and he rushed to the school, bursting into the examination hall and saying to the supervisor, 'I want Amin to come home now. There is a war on.' The supervisor dismissed his request: 'I don't think it is going to be war, just a skirmish in the desert.' 'Anyway, I want Amin out,' said Rafiq, 'and you can check with the consulate.' The supervisor did so and was told at once that all the boys should be sent home. As they left the hall, they could hear the sound of gunfire and the crashing of mortarshells.

I was always grateful that Rafiq acted so promptly, because not long after he left with Amin, some of the staff and students were caught up in the cross-fire. In no time we were in the midst of the conflict and in the utmost danger, especially in Beit Hanina where the houses with their vast glass windows were not made to withstand such a war. The shattered glass lay in heaps in the alleys and pathways, making walking anywhere very risky. Most of the houses had no air-raid shelters so that we had very little protection from the bombing.

We went down to our neighbours, Kamal and Mary and their four children. Rafiq had known Kamal since Bishop Gobat schooldays. He came from a Muslim Jerusalemite family and owned a hotel on the Mount of Olives. His wife Mary was Lebanese, brought up in the USA. That first night of the war, we all huddled in the corridor between two rooms. We were afraid, trapped and disillusioned. There was a bitter taste in our mouths. The children were our greatest concern, lying on blankets, clinging to us – or was it we to them? It was a sinister repeat of the Suez War. We heard shelling and gunfire. The electricity was cut. It was so frightening to wait in the dark, hearing the gunfire, fearing that the attackers might enter the house and shoot us all. Every now and then there would be an explosion of rockets fired by Israeli planes on the Jordanian army base in Shufat, two or three kilometres away from us, and on the Jordanian tanks and armoured cars retreating on the Jericho road.

In the early hours of the morning, Amin sneaked upstairs, crawling on all fours, while I called him to come back and shelter. From the bathroom window that overlooked the main street, he could see a column of Israeli tanks with Hebrew script on their sides. Amin had learnt a bit of Hebrew at St John's School in Haifa and he could hear the officers shouting orders in that language. When he came back downstairs, our landlord had called in to see how we were. He was one of the local voluntary guard. Amin ventured to say, '*Ammo* (Uncle – a polite form of address), I have just seen a column of Israeli tanks in the street. I saw the Hebrew writing and heard their language.' 'Silly boy!' He retorted angrily. 'What on earth are you saying?' He threw a fold of his *kaffiyeh* round his neck and walked out to the gateway. When he came back, he said triumphantly, 'Amin, you were wrong. They are the vanguard of the Iraqi troops.' The words went through me like an arrow. I had heard this before, remembering the Israeli invasion of Nazareth. Could the landlord have been mistaken, like the poor Nazareth woman who was shot long ago? I knew that Hebrew might sound like an Arabic dialect to those who do not know the language, especially if is spoken with a Sephardic (oriental) accent. Amin was silent. There was a lull. We went upstairs and from the windows overlooking the main street we saw a sight that left us in no doubt as to who had won. Armed to the teeth, driving their armoured cars through Beit Hanina, was an Israeli tank division. We heard that it drove on through Ramallah, Nablus and Jenin without meeting any resistance.

The wasteground by the Greek Catholic convent opposite our house now seethed with soldiers and tanks. We had been vanquished. Later, we heard about the utter defeat in Sinai. In a surprise attack on 5 June, Israel had destroyed most of the Egyptian airforce on the ground. Ten thousand of the Egyptian army lay dead and 13,000 captured. Jerusalem and the West Bank were under Israeli rule by 7 June and two days later they had taken the Suez Canal. On 10 June they occupied the Golan Heights, destroying the Syrian town of Kuneitra and driving out 17,000 of its inhabitants. Even after the cease-fire had been declared, Israel captured Mount Hermon, turning it into a listening-post. The Six-Day War was a victory for Israel, who had new territories, new sources of water. For the Arabs it was utter defeat. How did I feel? Perhaps I was the saddest, angriest person on the West Bank, not only because of the defeat in the war and the Arab disunity, but simply because I knew what was awaiting us. My experiences in Israel had taught me what lay ahead. It was like living a nightmare for the second time: land was seized, houses demolished, people were banished and families separated, settlements were built; people were imprisoned and tortured, or placed under house arrest. Peasants who had lived on their ancestral lands for generations were now evicted, their olive trees uprooted, their animals dragged out. Sometimes the animals persisted in returning to where their stables and pens had been.

There were the checkpoints on the road where you were stopped on your own soil by the occupier who could order you back under threat of punishment, and, what was in many ways worst of all, there was the crushing of a culture, a way of life, on the pretext of what had happened thousands of years ago. And this time the programme of cultural destruction would run more efficiently and ruthlessly since it had already been tried out on the first portion of Palestine.

The Western world hailed the genius of the Israeli generals. Some Protestant churches in Europe, especially in the Netherlands, rang their bells in jubilation. A half-page advertisement appeared in the *Jerusalem Post*, placed there by the head of the Lutheran Sisters of Darmstadt, thanking God for the victory of Israel over the Arab armies. In the days that followed we saw Israelis in their thousands rushing to the newly acquired land to celebrate in dance and song, stopping by a house where King Hussein used to stay where they lingered and took photographs. The victorious troops returned to Israel carrying a large portrait of the Jordanian king as war booty.

What of Nasser? On 9 June he announced his resignation, saying, 'Arab unity began before Nasser and will remain after him. I always told you that it is the nation that survives ... I am not liquidating the revolution, for it is not the property of one generation.' People took to the streets in Cairo, Beirut, Damascus, Baghdad, chanting his name, calling him to stay. Although the ship might go down, they still had confidence in the captain. The next day, the Egyptian National Assembly met to reject Nasser's resignation and voted him leader of 'the military and political rebuilding of the country'.

The June War was a great defeat for the Arabs of Egypt, Jordan, Syria and Lebanon, but it was worst for the Palestinians on the West Bank. Dispossessed for the second time, they fled across the Jordan river from the camps in Jericho and elsewhere – 150,000 new refugees starting another ordeal in Jordanian camps. Nobody could believe that Israel would stay on the West Bank. For the next few nights we took shelter with our neighbours again. A curfew was imposed. The bodies of soldiers and volunteer fighters lay scattered on the hills around Jerusalem, swelling with decay. Families began to run out of food. After a week it was announced that the curfew would be lifted for a few hours every afternoon. We ventured out and found spent cartridges and jagged glass everywhere. Our car had lost its windscreen and some of the panes of our veranda windows had been shattered, but apart from that we had survived unscathed.

Along the road to Jericho there were burnt out Jordanian tanks. When I later visited Jericho, the most depressing sight I saw was the camp of 'Aqabat Jaber. It had been targeted by bombs and flares and the 3,000 inhabitants had fled across the river before the Israeli army arrived. I saw the awkward, humble shacks standing empty, built for refugees who had been hoping that one day justice would prevail. There was something pathetic about those poor homes, now deserted, as if they were crying out, 'What else do you want to take?' Amin, meanwhile, had found his damaged bicycle and took it upon himself to go and look up those who might need visiting. He went to see two sisters, Asma and Basima Faris, friends of my mother living in Sheikh Jarrah, now a dangerous part of Jerusalem. They told me later how they had been sitting huddled by themselves when they heard a knock. 'Who is it?' they asked hesitantly. When Amin explained, they opened the door. 'I came to see that you are alright,' he said. '*Teita* (grandmother) was worried about you.'

The two sisters were stunned and very much afraid for Amin, thinking how foolish my mother was to send her grandson on such an errand. 'You must go home before the curfew resumes,' they said. 'You are the one in danger, Amin. Please go. Tell *Teita* we are alright.' But Amin's philanthropic mission did not stop there. Despite the state of his bicycle, he went on to Al 'Azeiryah, or Bethany, east of Jerusalem, where his cousin 'Afaf was working as a mental health nurse. By then, time was running out. 'Afaf was horrified to see Amin taking such a risk, but was very grateful for his visit because she had been cut off from her family in Ramallah.

Amin had told me that he was just going round the corner to see a friend, the son of a United Nations man. When he did not come back, I went to stand on the balcony, my heart burning, waiting for his return. Rafiq, optimistic as usual, was not sharing my fears: 'He will come. Stop worrying.' I left the balcony and threw myself on the bed. Where was my son? I went down to see Kamal and Mary and they too became very worried. The landlord said he would go and stand by the gate to watch out for him. Time ran out. The curfew began. Fifteen minutes passed. No Amin. They must have shot my son. Sure enough, in the dead silence of the curfew and not far from our house, we heard two shots. A few minutes later, Amin appeared, pale-faced, with his friend. They had been stopped by the army and the soldiers shot at them. When the other boy said he was the son of a UN worker, they mercifully released them.

One of Israel's policies was refusing to buy imports, especially food and consumer goods. All delicacies, clothes, electrical appliances and food were locally produced. When we first came to Jordan, we had found it a pleasant change to be able to buy things from the outside world. When the curfew was finally lifted after the June War, carloads of people rushed from Israel to empty the shops of the foreign goods – fridges, ovens, fabrics, tinned food – as well as to buy souvenirs of Arab culture, the carpets, silver and handicrafts. They paid low

prices with Israeli money which the vendors then had to exchange at a lower rate. Soon all that was left were Israeli goods,
and tins of peas and soup. Again, I was reminded of earlier
times, of the late 1940s and 1950s, the strict rationing, and
nothing but Israeli produce in the shops.

As early as 11 June, residents of Jerusalem's Maghrebi quarter were given notice to quit their houses before the bulldoz-
ing began to create a space facing the Wailing Wall. About a
thousand people were evicted by force from their homes, including a professor of Arabic whom I knew. He and his sisters
all lost their houses. Outside Jerusalem, the destruction of
villages began and some 20,000 houses were blown up in the
first ten years of Israeli occupation. We saw a house being
blown up in our neighbourhood. One day the landlord told us
to keep all our windows open: a house nearby was to be demolished. It was the home of the parents of a young man by the
name of William Nassar. They were ordered to get out in half
an hour. Trying to take as many of their possessions as they
could, they left hurriedly. The soldiers put dynamite at the
corners and the house collapsed, leaving the family with a
heap of stones and nowhere to go. They looked like people
standing around at a funeral, after the body has been buried.

On 22 November 1967, the UN Security Council unani-
mously passed Resolution 242 which demanded Israeli withdrawal from occupied territories. The omission of the word
'the' before the word 'territories' made the resolution ambiguous, causing much debate and giving Israel pretexts for
choosing the explanation which suited her. All the same, Israel
ignored the Resolution and on 16 December 1967 named the
West Bank Judea and Samaria. Then began a process of
settlement-building, despite the Security Council's condem-
nation of the acquisition of territory by war and emphasis on
the need to work for a just and lasting peace in which every
state in the area could live in safety. The most fearful aspect of
the occupation was the systematic encircling of Jerusalem by
fortress-shaped high-rise apartments, chains of formidable
house walls, besieging the Eastern part of the city. As you
came into Jerusalem, you saw buildings mushrooming everywhere and soon what had once been fields, olive gardens and
Arab houses was engulfed by Ramat Eshkol, Ramot and many
other Jewish settlements.

The economy stagnated. The integration of East Jerusalem into the Israeli economy resulted in the Arabs losing out because of restrictions on imports and exports, competition from Jewish enterprise, and new and higher taxes, as well as Israel's weak currency due to inflation. The population of the city changed rapidly. In 1947 the UN had envisaged the population of the Jerusalem area as almost equally distributed between Arabs (51%) and Jews (49%). Between 1967 and 1975 Israel settled 35,000 Jewish immigrants in the city.

Tourism became a highly sensitive subject. What would the guides tell visitors about the history, the ownership of the land? I remembered the neighbour of one of our Haifa parishoners who in 1950 told me that the Pope should encourage tourism to the Holy Land (which this neighbour called Israel), because they needed the money. Would West Bank Palestinians be allowed to work as guides? History, as we all discover, needs lots of fairness and objectivity. By ignoring certain periods or emphasizing others, you abuse the story of human experience. It was (and still is) disturbing that in the face of these policies, changing the face of Jerusalem and claiming it as solely Jewish – let alone throwing out the Palestinians and expropriating their land on the West Bank – the West preserved a wall of complacency, if not actually aiding Israel in fulfilling her plans. The Palestinians are the living stones, the ones who kept the faith in the Holy Land since the Day of Pentecost. Jerusalem is the capital of their country where many of them lived and practised their Christianity. Their Muslim compatriots also have religious claims on the city. The mystical flight of the Prophet from the Rock is as sacred to them as the Western Wall is to the Jews. It was to the Palestinians that the Jerusalem places of worship belonged, as Canterbury Cathedral belongs to the English, and Notre Dame to the French. If the West deemed it fit to regard Jewish beliefs as a justification for the return of the Jews, then surely there was far more cause not to turn out the Christians from the place where Jesus lived, died and was resurrected, and just as much reason not to bar the Muslims from their own highly revered shrine of the Aqsa Mosque and the Dome of the Rock.

The interaction between the indigenous people and the ecumenical community in Jerusalem is at the very essence of the Christian experience. Neither can live without the other.

The Christian West invested a lot in the Holy Land by way of hostels, convents, churches, schools, hospitals, orphanages and Bible institutes. These were acts of love, of coming together, which encouraged the indigenous church. Without that indigenous church, without Palestinian Christians, all that is left in the Holy Land are cold stones, empty shrines and academic ideas.

After the war, a woman writer called Elizabeth Elliot was commissioned by an American publisher to come to Israel and write about what had happened in 1967. She was one of five women whose husbands had been killed by the Auca tribespeople whom they had gone to befriend. Elizabeth had gone to meet the people who had killed her husband, Jim. She took her small daughter and spent a year with them, later writing her story in *Life* magazine in a series called 'The Savage is my Friend'. After arriving in Jerusalem and learning the Israeli side of the story, she was curious to know more about the Palestinian point of view. She interviewed some key people and then came to see me, asking, 'How would you explain the plight of your people to an ordinary American housewife?' I answered, 'How would this woman feel if somebody came and told her to leave her house and garden because they were not hers, because the newcomer had been there 2,000 years before?' The Palestinians were not only told but driven out, persecuted and named as terrorists, deprived of all human rights of birthplace and identity. I went on to explain how ignorant the West was about the Palestinians. As our conversation continued, she told me a little about her experiences with the Auca tribespeople, how she had found them to be a gentle, peace-loving community.

I later heard from her friends that the American publishers had refused to publish the book, because of the good things she wrote about the Palestinians. They had asked her to omit parts, but she had refused, saying that she had written what she saw and heard. The book later found another publisher and appeared as *The Furnace of God*.

13
Parents and Children

After Amin had finished his schooling, he was very keen to study abroad. We were helped by a young Englishman, Robert Likeman, whom we first met in Haifa and who now wrote on our behalf to his old school, St John's, in Leatherhead, Surrey. Amin got a scholarship at the age of sixteen: the flight from the nest had begun. We stood at Lydda airport, saying goodbye to our eldest son who was nervous at flying for the first time to a country he did not know. As we saw his plane getting smaller and smaller, like a bird disappearing beyond the horizon, the flight from the nest was no more a mere metaphor.

Robert and his wife Christine were like Amin's guardians and they gave us great and gracious assistance. For all the years that Amin was in England, their home was his. We kept in touch by regular letters which made all the difference to us. At one time, though, we did not receive any letters for a while. Being by nature prone to worry, my heart grew heavy. I went out on the veranda to find Karma crying. I had not told her of my fears for Amin, but when I asked what was wrong, she sobbed, 'It's Amin.' I tried to cheer her up, saying, 'Nothing is wrong. He is happy.' She replied, 'No, he is sick.' That day, the long-awaited next letter arrived. It was from Robert, starting with the bad news that Amin had a spot on his lung and had to stay in hospital, although the doctors said that his condition was not serious. I was a sad mother, unable to go and visit him because we could not afford the flight.

Amin's experiences in Beit Hanina had an echo in a prize-winning poem which he wrote at school which included the lines:

What crime have they done that once again, strangers in their land become?
And the world, haughty and dignified, moves her eyes to stare in wonder.

On the home front, domestic duties carried on as usual but we urgently required extra help as my mother needed care and my writing was taking up much of my time. After Naddiyeh's departure, I had three women, one after the other. None of them stayed long because of the dangerous and unstable times and the location of our house. One of these three women was Haniyah, a tall, fair-skinned girl with two thick plaits of golden hair. In her white scarf and embroidered dress she was lovely to look at, but even lovelier to know – peaceful, quiet, smiling, ready to do whatever was asked of her. In the afternoons, waiting for the bus home after her work was done, she would sit and embroider Palestinian designs on dresses for herself and for her family. She had to leave us shortly before the June War. I cannot remember why, but it probably had something to do with the family moving. I often wondered what happened to her.

Nearly six weeks after the end of the war, she came to pay us a visit. I was glad to see her, but was saddened to hear her news. I was asking her what had happened to her family and she told me that they had to move quickly from their house to a less dangerous place and how she had gathered up her valuables to take. 'What were you able to take, Haniyah?' I asked. I was shocked by her reply: 'You know, the little plastic boxes which people give out at weddings, and our plastic cooking utensils.' 'But what about your *thaub* (embroidered dresses)?' 'Oh, those! I left them behind. I can always embroider more.' 'But, Haniyah, those are the most precious things you own!' She looked at me, mystified at my reaction. 'How many did you leave?' I asked. 'Six or seven.' My shocked face made her add, 'Maybe you are right. I didn't think. All I knew was that I could make more dresses, but I could never replace those little boxes.'

Palestinian women have always worked very hard to keep alive the tradition of those beautiful symbols of our culture, the *thaub*. Widad Kawar, wife of my second cousin Kamil, toured the world with her collection of one thousand Palestinian dresses. I cannot forget Haniyah's dresses, though. The whole incident became a symbol of Third World countries shedding their natural and practical way of living and adopting Western ways, believing them to be more developed and never considering the consequences.

The second woman who came to help in our house was Fadwa, a red-haired, freckle-faced Christian who was married to a Muslim and who talked constantly. She came once a week and arrived unexpectedly on the second day after the initial lifting of the curfew. Who was ready to do house-cleaning in such a situation? The children were all at home, we had no bread but, seeing as she had come, I told her that she might as well do a little work. Fadwa went into my mother's room to make the bed. Later, when she had gone home, my mother called me, very upset. She had decided to keep her savings of 600 Jordanian pounds in a linen bag under her pillow because of the war situation, but now she could not find them. We looked everywhere but found nothing. We could not go after Fadwa because of the curfew and there was no government to whom we could put such a complaint, not when the whole country had been taken. The money was never recovered and Fadwa never came to work for us again.

For a very short time I had a woman called Um Halimeh. She was a refugee, newly arrived in Ramallah from Yalu, one of the three villages destroyed by the Israelis in the fertile valley near the Trappist Latroun monastery. Um Halimeh had a little daughter, about eight years old, who had suffered from polio and wore braces on her legs. Um Halimeh's husband had left her, going (she suspected) to a North African country, perhaps Libya. As well as her disabled child, she cared for her two elderly parents. She told me the story of how she was forced from her village: 'All of a sudden we saw tanks and soldiers. Some entered our house and told us that we had half an hour to leave. My mother, who was eighty, and I began to collect the things that we thought most valuable. Then we looked around and could not find my father. He was out in the orchard, moving from one tree to the other, bidding them farewell and crying.'

Um Halimeh repeated the folksong which her father had sung, her arms round her little girl who always accompanied her to our house:

You olive trees I planted
I shall never see you grow.
May the doves that come and go
Bring my *salaams* [love] to you.

May those who betrayed us
Be also betrayed.
I have never begged or asked for wealth,
But always had a roof over my head,
Yet at journey's end
I am homeless, a refugee, thrown out, despised.

She began to cry. I could not control my tears. Um Halimeh looked tragic. Suddenly she realized that she had made her child sad and wiped away her own tears. I remember her always encouraging her little daughter: 'Halimeh is a clever girl, of course she is. She ties her own braces. She tries to help me.' And she would hug her, holding her dark plaits in her hand, the plaits so well combed and braided that not one hair was out of place.

When Halimeh was sitting on the veranda by herself, and we were in the kitchen, Um Halimeh would tell the story of their journey on foot to Ramallah; they were thirsty and hungry, and she had to hold each of her parents by one arm, her daughter dragging along behind. Sometimes the little girl could not walk and her mother had to carry her for a while. Her father did not survive the trauma and died soon after, but her mother was still living.

After a while Um Halimeh stopped coming from the refugee camp. It was too much for her with all the checkpoints on the road and her disabled child who was by now going to school. What had left the greatest impression on her was that her old father had not bothered to take a single one of his belongings. 'All he wanted was to say goodbye to the orchard,' she would say in her country accent. 'See, Um Amin (for so she called me), can you imagine somebody who didn't bother to collect even his good cloak or his savings? Who, when he had so little time left, chose to walk in the orchard, looking at his trees and crying because he was losing them?'

It was through the efficiency and dedication of its board members that the YWCA in Jerusalem could rise to meet the challenge of the distressing situation after the 1967 war. Their entire programme became geared to rehabilitation, vocational training, meeting visitors, boosting the morale of the crushed people and holding ecumenical services which were always happy occasions, involving all the different Jerusalem communities. They reached out to their compatriots, to those in the refugee camps, and tried to explain the Palestinian tragedy to fellow members coming from abroad. Many board members held key posts in the community, many of them voluntary. There was Betty Majaj, matron of the Maqasid Hospital and later director of the Princess Basma Rehabilitation Centre on the Mount of Olives. She is a tireless, gracious Lebanese lady who was pleased to show me round her workplace when I visited the centre. In one room there were small, high beds where little boys were sitting, their sunburnt faces smiling, their dark eyes laughing. I forgot their disabilities until I saw the wheelchairs near each little bed. Years later, in the *Intifada* uprising of December 1989, Betty worked to help those shot by the Israeli army. (*Intifada* means shaking off, and in this context, the shaking off of fear and the start of an uprising against a harsh military rule.)

After showing me the centre and telling me about the difficulties of raising enough money to cover the costs, Betty took me out on to the balcony, overlooking the Mount of Olives, and there I saw row after row of houses belonging to the Israeli settlement called *Ma'alot Adomim*, built on expropriated land and stretching to the Jericho road, to what is called in Arabic *Al-Khan el-Ahmar*, supposedly the place where the Good Samaritan helped the man who fell among robbers. Very near the YWCA was *Dar e-Tifil* ('House of the Child') where Hind Husseini, a member of the prominent Muslim Husseini family, established a shelter for orphaned Palestinian children in 1948. I used to visit her and be shown round the place where they lived and received schooling in a happy atmosphere, with Mama Hind like a loving, jealous mother for the children of Palestine who had lost parents, home and land, but not heart and hope. Hind was helped by her Christian friend Basima Faris.

I knew many other people who worked tirelessly and sacrificially to ease the plight of the West Bank refugees, opening family centres, teaching preventative medicine, childcare and nutrition, and caring for the disabled. What could a farmer do when separated from his fields and resettled among stony hills? What hope was there for the village cut off from its water supply? The children with a war-zone now dividing them from their school? I remember people like Lizy Nasir, Dr Salwa Khoury 'Ottaqi, Basima Faris, Hind Husseini, Elias Khoury and his wife Summaya, and many others. They tried to give people back their dignity, their identity, although they had lost homes, land and nationhood. I think with special fondness of Sameeha el-Khalil whose courage and vision gave hope to many women in the Ramallah area.

The Day of Karameh

On 21 March 1968, the Israeli army crossed the border into Jordan and attacked the Shuneh Karameh area with a force of 9,000 armoured troops grouped into three brigades, and about 1,200 infantry, as well as air cover. The aim was to destroy the *fedayeen* fighting force (freedom fighters) called *'Asifa* (storm) and the Jordanian army. We heard about the attack and were expecting the worst. I was sitting with Mary and Kamal, talking about what new calamity might be awaiting us, when Kamal commented that it was strange how the Israeli force had not yet come back victorious. We heard later that although they had planned a surprise attack, the *fedayeen* and the Jordanian army were prepared and fought back.

The Jordanian artillery kept the tank columns from the Allenby Bridge while Abu Sharif, the *'Asifa* commander, led a section to ambush the Israelis in banana groves near the river. Karameh itself was a large refugee camp. Most of the inhabitants had already left but around 300 put up fierce resistance to the invaders and the fighting was hand to hand. The name *Karameh* means dignity. To this day, Jordan keeps 21 March as the Day of Karameh in memory of the bravery and unity of Jordanians and Palestinians.

14
Home on the
West Bank

On Sunday 2 March 1969, at 1.30 am, Israeli soldiers raided the vicarage of the Revd Elia Khoury, vicar of St Andrew's Anglican church in Ramallah. They arrested him, searched his house and moved him to an unknown place. They then closed the church and locked the outer gate. When the parishioners came for morning prayer and found the churchyard gate closed, they gathered in the main street to say prayers and sing hymns. Supporters from other different denominations and religions joined them. Archbishop Appleton and Bishop Qubain contacted different ecclesiastical authorities as well as Israeli officials, to try and sort out the situation. The WCC and the Archbishop of Canterbury attempted to intervene, but Moshe Dayan, then in command of the West Bank, chose to banish Mr Khoury. He left the West Bank for Jordan, where he received a very warm welcome, and was later elected Assistant Bishop in Amman.

Before these events, Archbishop Appleton had suggested that Rafiq should be appointed Canon Residentiary of St George's Cathedral. Due to internal church politics, however, this appointment had been delayed. Now, owing to the detention and banishment of Elia Khoury, Bishop Qubain had no alternative but to ask Rafiq to take over the pastoral work in Ramallah. His duties covered Ramallah itself and two villages to the north: Bir Zeit, where the university is, and 'Abboud, a small village near Ramallah which has remains of several Byzantine churches. His work also included serving as chief judge in the ecclesiastical court (since Turkish times, governments in the Middle East had given religious communities legal rights over matters of personal status, such as marriage, divorce and inheritance).

I was sorry to leave the house in Beit Hanina and weary at the thought of taking down the curtains, packing the furniture, piling kitchen utensils in boxes. I felt I had not lived there long enough to enjoy it fully, although I can still remember the view from my bedroom window, the quiet, the sense of belonging again in a culture. We arrived in Ramallah with two trucks and our car, parking in the churchyard. As I got out, I felt unable to face the prospect of setting up home in yet another new place. My health was not at its best, either. I was suffering from arthritis and from another as yet undiagnosed condition which made me exhausted and gave me pain all over my body, especially in my limbs. I do not think I left a good impression on my neighbours whose idea of a good housewife was a woman bursting with energy and organizational skills.

We found the atmosphere of the town a mixture of heaviness, panic and defiance. The vicarage and its yard were surrounded by buildings and looked claustrophobic though homely. I took comfort from a tall, solitary pine tree which grew opposite the house. I used to look at it from the window as it swayed in the breeze, and wonder if it had been a sapling when I was young. My uncle had been the vicar of the church in Ramallah for many years, living in the old vicarage with his family. In those days, it had been surrounded by pine and almond trees and I remember visiting it during my school holidays, as a very young child, and seeing the roof of the house covered with drying almonds.

Opposite our house, in a ground floor flat, lived two sisters who were both active in the church committees and helpful to the incumbent. One sister had a club foot, but she was always a happy, courageous, entertaining person who spent hours sitting outside her flat, surrounded by many varieties of fuchsia plants. The sisters had a lot of friends who visited frequently, sitting in the churchyard and drinking coffee together.

The old vicarage adjacent to the church had been turned into a church hall, housing the activities of the youth club and the women's committee. Above it were two other flats where my sister-in-law had been living with her family since the 1960s. Near them were another Anglican family and above us were two more. We lived cordially alongside one another, respecting our mutual need for space and privacy. There was a small garden in front of our house which our friend Farahan M'arouf supplied with plants and seedlings from his flower shop and nurseries. He also contributed generously with flowers for the church on Sundays. Our house, like the one in

Beit Hanina, had a beautiful long veranda with glass windows which I filled with my calico curtains. The veranda faced the common yard and had a full-length stone windowsill. I covered this windowsill with African violets to which I had become addicted. At one time I had thirty-six pots of them in different shades of lilac, pink and white, as well as other plants. I also used the windowsill to display my brass trays and vases. On one side of the veranda we had a niche with a big picture of Jesus saying, 'Let the little children come to me'. Ramallah is very cold in winter, so we covered the floor with two identical striped rugs in blue, red and white, and kept warm by lighting a coal fire in our brazier stove.

My mother loved the veranda, and so did Rafiq, especially when he learnt to play backgammon with some friends. On Sundays after church, the men would occupy the veranda, while the women would sit inside. Before going to the service, I would prepare my little coffee cups for Arabic coffee. By now they were not full sets, as some had broken, but they were a collection from bygone times. My neighbour (who would say anything to anybody) said to me, 'Here you are good for nothing except making coffee.' I think she had real insight, because I really became alive when I made Arabic coffee. It was nostalgic – it brought me something deep, a sense of security, a reminder of the life of my ancestors.

After our move, we realized that commuting to Jerusalem was hazardous and time-consuming for the children because of the army checkpoints, and so Karma moved from Schmidt School to the Friends' Girls' School. Randa, who had only one more year before graduating, asked to become a boarder. Nabil still went every day on the bus, as he was also finishing his last year at St George's. Amin was, of course, in England.

Graduation day is very important for families on the West Bank. It is a special day not only for the graduates and parents but for the whole community. Local dignitaries would be invited, as well as religious leaders. I had missed my own graduation day because of the political situation at the time, and I had also missed my brother's and my elder son's, so it was a great day for us when we attended Nabil's graduation from St George's.

Randa graduated from Schmidt School in a dress of Thai silk, material brought back by Rafiq from a visit to Thailand.

We managed to get her a college place at the Beirut University College (BUC). Amin wanted his brother to join him at Swansea University in the UK, where he was now studying electrical engineering. We did not like the idea because of financial difficulties. To my surprise, however, I managed to get a job as headmistress of Talitha Kumi, a German Christian day school for girls in Beit Jala, the sister town of Bethlehem, which helped pay the fees for my boys' education. I had to leave home at 6.00 am in order to get to the school through all the military checkpoints on the road.

Although it was sad for Karma not to continue at Schmidt School, which offered a more comprehensive syllabus than most, including the chance to study German, the Friends' Girls' School was very good. Founded by the Quakers in 1860, under the direction of the Revd Eli and Sybil Jones, it had a different approach, encouraging freedom of expression. It was very near our Ramallah house, but even that did not prove much safer. Any show of resistance in the town resulted in Israeli soldiers breaking into schools, beating students, following those who managed to flee and picking them up, in the main street, in the alleys, even when they managed to hide behind garden hedges. Their school uniforms attracted the soldiers' attention. The girls wore a dress or skirt under their navy uniforms and many times Karma came home with her uniform hidden in a bag, leaving her school satchel back in her desk.

The military government on the West Bank closed the schools and universities for long periods, frequently disrupting education for all students including girls like my daughters. It was a very happy occasion for me when Karma finally graduated. The ceremony took place in Dr Tautah Hall in the Friends' Boys' School. I remember Ramallah's fine architecture, its beautiful gardens, its trees, on that day. It was a day so like the old Palestinian days and that, together with my daughter graduating after years of learning, made the whole experience deeply gratifying and joyful. Karma then went on to study at Bir Zeit University.

Bir Zeit village, eleven kilometres north of Ramallah, became famous after a national school was founded there in 1924 by Miss Nabeeha Nasir. This school developed into a secondary school, then a college and later still a university. It still nurtures the Palestinian dream of a free state and places special emphasis on our national identity and culture. Among its remarkable professors is Dr Hanan Ashwari, and it remains a powerhouse, a lighthouse on the West Bank. In 1994 my granddaughter Reema left her home in Swansea, UK, to spend a year studying there. Bir Zeit lay within the area of Rafiq's pastoral care and I often went there with him. The road between Ramallah and Bir Zeit was very beautiful, especially in the spring, when the valleys and rolling hills were studded with poppies, cyclamen, anemones and wild daisies. In Bir Zeit, we used to visit the lovely family home of Musa Nasir, a friend of my uncle's family from Nablus days. Musa Nasir's sister, Wadieh, was a friend of my mother's and it was fascinating to watch when the two of them were reunited after nearly fifty years. The years dropped away as they started to share memories of the old times.

Musa Nasir's nephew was the Christian Palestinian poet Kamal Nasir who joined the PLO and became its mouthpiece. In 1973 he was found shot and mutilated in Beirut, along with two other PLO leaders. The news was devastating, not only for his immediate family, but for the whole of the West Bank. Rafiq was due to conduct the funeral service, but Israel closed the approaches to Bir-Zeit, and Rafiq had to argue his way through the heavy military presence to get to the church. Kamal Nasir had devoted his life and poetry to the cause of his people, depicting their concerns and frustrations, at times optimistic, at times desperate. After the funeral service, we walked back to the family house and gathered in a circle in the garden, listening to speakers paying tribute to the martyr. Armed Israeli soldiers stood nearby. It was spring and the breeze was fresh, the grass green, the flowers blooming. To me it felt symbolic, that the spirit of the dead poet was still free, and now beyond the power of chains and prison bars.

15
Crossing Bridges

Ramallah was like Nablus, one of the major cities of the West Bank with many villages clustered around. I should call it Ramallah-Bireh, although there are now no boundaries between what were once two separate towns. The Ramallah which I remember was a city of orchards, famous for its fig trees and vines, the red roofs nestling among verdant valleys, the old houses reflecting the life of an agricultural society, of families close to each other. Ramallah people, like those in many provincial towns and villages, retained the history of their families and lived by the standards and traditions of the past. The city was blessed in terms of schools and education. Besides the Friends' schools, there was a good school run by the Roman Catholics and the Women's Training College founded by UNWRA. Later, our church was to sponsor the evangelical homes for both boys and girls. The excellent education produced many talented and free thinkers in Ramallah. From the turn of the century, Ramallah people had emigrated in their hundreds to the States looking for work, but they never forgot their pretty home city nestling in the hills. They always came back to the family home, either to repair it or to build another house.

Israel's occupation smashed the idyll. Our Ramallah years were ones of oppression for the Palestinians on the West Bank. The military government had its headquarters in the Taggart building in the city . The central square, Al Manara, was the scene of frequent and tragic confrontations between unarmed civilians and the occupying army. Hundreds of people had to squat each day outside the government building to get a permit either to cross the bridge to Amman or to be allowed to see family members who were under arrest.

Before the occupation, it had taken the people of Amman an hour to get to Jericho, where they spent the day in the winter resort and then went home. When the Israeli military government took over, orders were issued forbidding anybody to cross the border without a permit from the military governor. Getting the permit depended on the recommendation of *Shin Bet*, the security service. Crossing the bridge became a most difficult, time-consuming and tiring procedure for us. People had to strip under the supervision of a military officer, piles of travellers' shoes were carried away in boxes, the heels pulled out and the shoe passed under electronic surveillance equipment. We would sit in a circle, shoeless, the women in one circle, the men in another, waiting for the mound of footwear to be returned. Sometimes you would find one shoe and fail to find the other.

The inspection of suitcases and carrier bags was no less rigorous, with every item pulled out and shaken, even if it was lingerie, make-up, toothpaste, or medicine. On one occasion they confiscated from me vital medicines which I had to take regularly for a heart condition. Once emptied, the suitcases were put in plastic bags and taken off for examination and any letters and photographs would be examined in a different section. Hundreds of us would be sitting and waiting, humiliated, from all walks of life. I felt especially sorry for the truck drivers who had to wait with their loads of fruit and vegetables in the scorching heat of Jericho – sometimes 38° or 40° centigrade. How many times I had to make that crossing, dreading each occasion; I who had endured the Mandelbaum Gate was now faced with the agony of the Allenby Bridge.

In my writing, such experiences lingered on, claiming their place in my stories. In my most recent collection at that time, *The Uprising of the Birds*, the stories all portrayed aspects of the horrendous injustice done to my people, facing Western Zionism backed by ruthless power and racist nationalism. One of the stories, 'A Letter at the Bridge', was based on an actual incident at the offices of Middle East Transport in Amman. Three grieving men approached the passengers, pleading with them to carry a short, urgent letter to a family in Nablus, reporting the death of their son, a university student, in a car accident in Cairo and telling them that the body would be taken to the bridge. They wanted to be sure that the family of the deceased would be there to receive the coffin. Nobody was prepared to carry the message, knowing the trouble they would face for trying to take written material across the bridge.

When the men approached me, I said I would deliver the message by word of mouth, but they insisted that the letter contained too many practical details. As I took my seat in the taxi and the wheels started to turn, I looked out at the three desolate men and suddenly stretched out my hand, saying, 'Give me the letter.' I was conscience-stricken that I had refused to offer such small assistance to my countrymen. They rushed towards the car, thanking me and assuring me that they would never forget my good deed.

I clutched the paper, dreading the bridge. Why did I not learn the letter by heart and throw it away? I could not. At the bridge it was even worse than I had feared. Everyone was given back their papers after they had been examined, and then suddenly I was summoned to an office where I saw three men sitting behind piles of paper and machines. One addressed me, 'What is this letter you are carrying?' 'It was given to me by some men to inform the parents of the death of their son.' 'Do you know these people?' 'No, I don't.' 'On what grounds are you carrying a letter from people you do not know?' 'I carried it on humanitarian grounds.' The questioning began to become Kafka-esque, suspicious, even more bureaucratic. 'How do you know that the contents are true?' 'I am sure they are. Anyway, the body will pass this bridge and you will find out the truth for yourselves.' 'Suppose it is a trick and the body is hiding a time-bomb?' I was growing very tired. I said, 'I do not think on these lines. I did what anyone would do in such a situation.' They consulted each other and at last handed the letter back. I went out with a great sense of relief, but I was also angry and confused. I reached the outer gate, impatient to get out of the inspection area into relative freedom. I handed my pass to the officer at the gate. It was not signed.

I went back, expecting the worst – the office might be closed, they might be planning more questioning – but I was lucky. My paper was signed and I joined the taxi full of passengers like me who had all been through similarly harsh treatment. I had been told to give the letter to somebody in the offices of the Department of Electricity in Jerusalem. The taxi-driver was kind and came with me to hand over the letter. Next day, the newspaper carried the obituary of the young man who had been killed in Cairo, and the details of his burial.

I felt sad, but at least the young man would be able to rest in the soil of his own country.

You will never understand the extent of the Palestinian frustration and anger until you put yourself in our shoes: waking up one morning to find that you have to get a permit to walk on your own land, to find bulldozers coming to demolish your house, to discover that the army have carried out a raid on your son's university and taken him away – and you would never know where he had gone. Often, in such a case, the verdict would be 'administrative arrest'. Palestinians came to dread such a verdict more than any other. 'Administrative arrest' meant that the military authorities could interrogate your son in whatever manner they chose, inflicting torture for as long as they wished.

The Ramallah I knew was in a continuous state of tension, like all the other cities on the West Bank. Collective punishment, youngsters being rounded up, imprisonment, administrative detention, destruction of homes – civilians had to face all this even in their work, schools and offices. One mother, a villager from Deir Dubwan, told me how they took her younger son and put him in a room near to where his elder brother was imprisoned, beating and kicking the older boy so that his brother would hear his screams and confess to what the other had never committed. A shopkeeper near the vicarage was arrested one day. It was hard for the neighbourhood to comprehend what had happened. He had always supplied us with groceries – a harmless man, not always in good health. Anxiously, we kept asking for information from his son who had taken charge of the business. He would simply shake his head.

The realization of the facts of our daily life left us in great shock, frustration and disbelief. Daily life became intolerable. We were captives in our own land. Our days fluctuated between the ordinary, the worries of any household anywhere, and the horrendous, when we had the status of captives, victims of unbridled cruelty and obsessive power.

In 1968, attempts were made to prepare a new translation of the Bible in Arabic. Rafiq and I were invited to a workshop at Christ Church, Jerusalem, where the project was to be discussed with an English specialist. At lunch-time, we went to the hostel in the church compound and joined an American tourist group at a table in the dining-room. Near me sat a man with a kind face and a long beard. 'And where do you come from?' he asked me. To evade all the questions that might ensue, I answered, 'I come from here. I am a Palestinian Arab.' 'Palestinian?' he repeated, looking unpleasantly surprised. 'Do you mean to say you are from the people who hijack planes?' 'I come from a people whose whole country has been hijacked for the last twenty-five years, while the world did not lift a finger in protest,' I replied. He shook his head and then said, as if thinking aloud, 'I could understand what you were saying, if it were not for the Bible!' 'And what is written in the Bible?' 'You know . . . that God had promised his chosen people the land and that they would return after exile.' 'Sorry, sir,' I said. 'I do not believe in a God that prefers one people to another. I do not believe that the God who created this vast universe has nothing to do except guard a piece of land. God is the father of all creation, a God of love.'

A man sitting opposite me, listening, turned out to be the leader of the group. He invited me to come and speak to them in the lobby over coffee. I did so, telling them about my inter-view with Elizabeth Elliot, explaining that ignorance is dan-gerous, especially when the ignorant are as powerful as the people of America. I told them about the Arab Christians, and spoke about the Israeli military rule. A woman wearing wide, printed silk trousers and a silk top came up to me, putting one hand on her hips and asking, 'Do you claim to be Christian?' 'Yes, God willing.' 'I'll tell you what you should do, then,' she went on. 'You must give up your house and garden to the Jews because that is what the Bible says must happen.' 'Would you give up your own house and garden?' I asked. She marched away angrily – but on the following Sunday, many members of that group, including the leader, came to our church. After the service they had coffee with us and with the members of the congregation, hearing more of our story. Some said that what they heard completely changed their thinking about the situation.

Early on the morning of 28 September 1970, I opened the front door and saw as usual my two neighbours sitting outside on their stone seat. Instead of sipping their morning coffee, they were crying. 'What's the matter?' I asked. 'Haven't you heard? Nasser is dead.' I could not believe it at first. Other neighbours came out, all in tears. We stood in the little vicarage yard, a bereaved, vanquished group. I went back to tell Rafiq the bad news and found that he had already heard. The Revd 'Audeh Rantisi, director of the Evangelical Boys' Home in Ramallah, came and he and Rafiq rang the church bell. All over the town we could hear other bells answering the sad tolling and in the minaret, the muezzin was chanting Koranic texts, praying for the dead president.

Nasser was buried the next day and it is said that five million people walked in the funeral procession. History may prove that he made many mistakes, but he was a breath of fresh air to the Arab world which had lain incapacitated after 400 years of Turkish rule.

Life in Ramallah

Ramallah was well known for its Palestinian cross-stitch embroidery. Many Palestinian villages and towns had their distinctive patterns and Ramallah had its own *Fellahi* (peasant-like) designs. With the refugee camps scattered all over the West Bank, women's organizations set out to help the refugees help themselves by forming co-operatives and paying the women for their embroidery work. It happened that Archbishop Appleton visited Kalandia camp and donated some money to the embroidery section. An UNWRA officer came to tell me that the Archbishop had sent a letter suggesting that I might be able to suggest ways of promoting the work. I went with him to Kalandia camp and met the two young women in charge of the embroidery. It was gorgeous, but very few people had the chance to see it.

I talked to the field director in the West Bank, Mr Bakrajian, an Armenian Jerusalemite, about where we could exhibit the work. 'Why not exhibit it with other Palestinian artefacts? Even furnish a whole room Palestinian-style?' I suggested. We found a house to rent and a whole team of workers came together from the UNWRA and YMCA vocational schools in Jericho to set up the exhibition. A committee was formed to buy Hebron glass, Jerusalem pottery, and brass trays. I did not do any of the practical work and the success of the exhibition was entirely thanks to Mr Bakrajian, Vera Tamari, 'Aisha and Fatima (who taught embroidery in the camps), to the vocational school students, but most of all to the young refugee girls who sat on the steps of their shabby one-room camp shacks, labouring to create this spot of beauty.

The young carpenters made shelves of carved wood for displaying the pottery and the glassware, and little lamps which shed a dim light, reflecting on the carved wood. There were divans with embroidered cushions, a huge brass tray on an oriental stand, shawls and carpets, plants in oriental holders. The dresses hung on the walls, robes fit for queens. It was like a scene from the Arabian Nights. I do not think it stayed in that house for long, but went to be housed in the refugee camp. That was where it belonged and I hope it is still there.

Although it is not my concern to discuss church politics, my story would be incomplete if I did not mention some of the developments taking place, and Rafiq's role in them. The Church was going through the period of restructuring which I have already described, and the Archbishop of Canterbury, who still had authority over the see of Jerusalem, asked the diocesan synod to choose four names from which he would select the bishop and assistant bishop of the restructured diocese. Since Rafiq was the second in seniority in the area, and because of his experience, he was sure that his name would be submitted – but it was not. He could not understand why, especially because at that time the number of clergy in the diocese was no more than twenty and Rafiq was one of the most highly qualified who led a minority church in Israel. Eventually, we found out that intense lobbying had taken place to exclude his name for a variety of reasons which I will not elaborate on here. Other disappointments were to follow. We were reminded, yet again, that the church is still made up of mere human beings. I should mention that none of it affected Rafiq, who was never ambitious for glory or prestige, and he never grew bitter or ceased being friendly to those who became his seniors. He worked till the very end in a way which was co-operative, happy, accepting, doing what he had to do with humour and trust.

Life dragged on in Ramallah. We carried out our daily duties, moving like people without expectations, fearing to hope for anything, as hopes had so often been shattered. Then a day came which started like any other, the day of a Jewish holiday called Yom Kippur, the Day of Atonement, 6 October 1973. Yom Kippur was the only day when Israeli radio was traditionally silent, but on that particular day Rafiq noticed that they were broadcasting classical and military music and commented how strange this was. Something must have happened. Before long, we heard exactly what it was. Three divisions of the Egyptian army had crossed Suez and captured the supposedly well defended Bar-Lev line. The little compound where we lived burst into life, everybody out in the yard, some listening to the radio, some going to the gate to find that neighbours down the street had also run outside in disbelief at the news.

A force of 500 Syrian tanks and two infantry divisions had also advanced into the Syrian territory captured in 1967 by Israel. Moshe Dayan was in despair until the United States rushed to the aid of Israel with an airlift of sophisticated weapons. The outcome of the war swung in Israel's favour and on 15 October they made a thrust across the Suez Canal between the second and third Egyptian divisions and consolidated a bridgehead on the west bank of Suez. As we followed the development of the war, we heard about the Arab use of the 'oil weapon'. The Organization of Arab Petroleum Exporting Countries (OPEC) met on 17 October in Kuwait and decided that its members should reduce oil production by 5 per cent a month until Israel withdrew from all occupied Arab territories. The Palestinians felt more confident that they were not after all forsaken, but the situation soon became more than an Arab–Israeli war. It became a clash of the superpowers.

America and the Soviet Union agreed to push for a cease-fire, demanding the implementation of UN Resolution 242 of 22 November 1967, calling on Israel to withdraw from the West Bank. Israel broke the cease-fire by trying to cut off the Egyptian third army in Suez and our excitement waned as we watched the ambiguous peace missions of Henry Kissinger and saw President Sadat of Egypt lose esteem as the war dwindled into troop disengagement agreements with a UN force in between. We had hoped that new horizons of justice and human rights would open before us, but instead we were faced with bilateral peace agreements between Egypt and Israel.

While living through such momentous political developments, we had a phone call from our son Amin, at Swansea University, surprising us with the news that he was getting married on 20 October to a young woman named Carole. We were very surprised because he was still a student and only twenty-two years old. He asked us to attend the wedding but this was impossible because of the October war. On 20 October at the time when the wedding would have been taking place, I invited our neighbours round for coffee and Arabic sweets. As I thought of Amin, far away, I could not restrain a tear now and then. It was not until a year later that we saw Amin with Carole and their new-born baby Reema. I got on very well with my daughter-in-law and Reema was the most beautiful baby – almond-shaped dark eyes, ivory skin, silken black hair. It was a great day when she was baptized by Rafiq and we invited our families over from Shefamr and Haifa, including Rafiq's parents – Reema's great-grandparents.

16
Dark Clouds and Sunshine

Our decision to move to Beirut in January 1977 may well mystify the reader of this story. It still mystifies me now. I could have said, 'No!' when Rafiq told me that the Church Council asked if he was willing to go. I can still see my neighbour coming down the stairs to our common yard, practically shouting at me when she heard of our decision: 'You must be mad. Who on earth see the flames burning and throw themselves into it?'

To get to Lebanon we would have to cross three boundaries – the occupied West Bank, the Jordan–Syrian border, and the Syrian–Lebanese border – and it would be impossible to take our furniture with us. Full of regrets, I said goodbye to my few nice pieces of furniture, and also my beautiful house-plants.

My mother was in no state to cross the Allenby Bridge. We contacted the Red Cross on both sides and they arranged for one car from the West Bank to get her to the bridge, accompanied by myself, and another to come from Amman. When the day came, however, we found ourselves stuck on the bridge as one of the officers had forgotten to sign a paper on our behalf in Jerusalem. Eventually the car did arrive from Amman, but our troubles did not end there. On arriving in Amman, I discovered that I had not brought the address and phone number of the house where we would be staying. Rafiq had the details but he was travelling separately in a taxi. The Red Cross car went in circles round the streets of Amman until we tracked down the right place. We had two nights' rest in Amman, and then the three of us flew to Beirut.

The taxi that took us from the airport to our new destination drove through streets lined with puckered, deserted houses, through alleys and roads of destroyed homes, mangled cars laid on the side, areas where shacks and temporary homes had been set up for refugees who had fled the latest attack, the squalor and garbage all around. Strange, bewildered broken faces looked at us for a fleeting second, then they were gone, like ghosts gloomy and foreboding. My heart fell, I remembered my neighbours' anger and blame for accepting to come to a place of death and suffering. I remember the sense of guilt I felt towards my family for bringing them to such a place.

My first impression of our new house was of a spacious living-room with large French windows. The house was newly whitewashed and had three balconies, a study and two bedrooms as well as the living-room. It belonged to a well-to-do Greek Orthodox Lebanese man, who lived with his family on the top floor. The church had rented it for the resident vicar and the previous occupant had been Samir Kafity, now Bishop in Jerusalem. When I set out my pottery, pictures, embroidery, and Hebron glass, and hung the pictures, and arranged the carpets, I began to feel as if it was home.

My reveries were broken by the column of Syrian tanks and the shooting out in the streets. All would have been well if times had been peaceful and Beirut still one of the jewels of the Mediterranean, but the very air was ominous. Destruction and the threat of imminent death lay all about us. Syrian troops had moved in to keep the peace after the civil war erupted in 1975, killing 50,000 in the first twelve months. Our house was exposed to danger by its very location, being in a sensitive part of the beleaguered city, opposite the American University Hospital (AUH).

The convulsions in the land of Palestine had had a profound impact on Lebanon, a small country which had always been a mosaic of minority cultures and religious groups existing in precarious relationship. When the Palestinians were pushed out of their own country, they flocked to the neighbouring Arab countries, including Lebanon. Some were the rich élite of Haifa who made Beirut their base, contributing to the wealth and progress of the city with their capital and business expertise. The majority had lost everything and came with empty hands – about 104,000 of them. They settled in fifteen refugee camps and while their numbers doubled, their fortunes did not, and they became unwanted second-class citizens. Technically entitled to reside in Lebanon, they remained officially stateless, a source of cheap labour and a focus of conflict among the Lebanese themselves. New waves of refugees arrived after the 1967 war, and after the troubles of 1970–71 in Amman. They met with harassment from the police and security forces and were disqualified from receiving state benefits. Seeing no sign of a solution to their situation, they began to organize themselves, taking their destiny into their own hands.

The Lebanese establishment, particularly the Maronite Christian leadership, viewed these developments with anger and mistrust, arguing that their activities against Israel would draw bloody reprisals. Their anger was further fuelled by the 1969 Cairo Agreement which regulated relations between the PLO and the Lebanese Government, brokered by Nasser, which ceded Lebanese sovereignty in parts of the south to the PLO to carry on its 'war of liberation'. Ultimately, the Palestinians became the catalyst which hastened a conflict already in the making.

The Extraordinary City

As Rafiq began his work, caring for the spiritual and physical welfare of the people and trying to alleviate their plight, we encountered the sense of horror and disbelief at the recent massacre of Palestinians at the refugee camp of Tel a-Z'atar after a seven-week siege. Children, women, and old people had been killed mercilessly, sometimes literally torn to pieces. Two thousand were killed and another few thousand left wounded. As I visited people and heard eye-witness accounts of the atrocities, I could not make sense of such savagery. I little knew that the situation would grow worse than even the most pessimistic forecasts. It was in March 1977, when we were still settling in Beirut, that we heard that Kamal Jumblatt, leader of the Druzes and founder of the Progressive Socialist Party, had been assassinated. The news was brought to us by Um Michel, our cleaning lady. Her face was pale and she shook both hands in a gesture of foreboding, saying, '*Allah ustur*' (May God keep us from what might befall us). After she left us that morning, the shops began to close and people hurried back to their homes, fearful, despairing. Cars rushed through the streets in all directions, and we heard shooting. A grey gloom hung over the city, as the people braced themselves for days of trouble. Later, we heard news of bloodshed, with Druzes attacking Christian villages and suffering counter attacks.

Meanwhile, a Geneva conference on peace in the Middle East was held, leading to a joint US-Soviet statement of the need to resolve the Palestinian question, agreeing that Israel should withdraw from the territories seized in 1967 and mentioning the legitimate rights of the Palestinian people. At last there was hope, but how quickly it was crushed. Israel's fierce opposition, and a protest involving 8,000 telephone calls and telegrams, led President Carter to abandon the initiative. Then came the bombshell: Anwar e Sadat, President of Egypt, was to visit Jerusalem on 19 November 1977. Most of the Arab world watched in dismay and disbelief, and many did not sleep that night, considering his decision a personal slap in the face. Next day the very walls of Beirut, like the morning papers, were full of anger and contempt. 'You fool, Sadat. We shall throw you in the rubbish bin of history' were the words I saw splashed in bright red on one wall. With the mediation of President Carter, the Camp David accords were signed between Israel and Egypt on 17 September 1978. By thus securing the Egyptian–Israeli border, the agreements allowed Israel to divert all its military might to the war in Lebanon.

Also in 1978 came the disappearance and presumed murder of Musa e-Sadr, the Shi'ite Muslim imam who had founded *Amal* (Hope), an armed group which was enthusiastically supported by the impoverished Shi'ite community of Beirut, in the face of a government who neglected them and remained unwilling to protect the south of the country against Israel's ruthless reprisals. The Shi'ites mourned Musa e-Sadr, plastering the streets with posters of him. Also their allegiance turned to Khomeini's Iran and the Ayatollah's picture appeared everywhere. In the small lift in our apartment block, I found posters for *HizbuAllah* (Party of God) and saw the group's members in the streets, angry, bearded young men.

As the political factions sub-divided and multiplied, each of the streets of Beirut became a world of its own. If it were not for the slogans on the walls, acting like road signs, you would have needed a map to know under which warlord's power each area lay – but even that knowledge would not keep you from the danger of stray bullets or random explosions.

Most days there was no water or electricity. Telephones were cut off most of the time, and many evenings there was nothing to do except sit at home. Candles were very much in demand and shops and small businesses would install their own generators. The noise of these machines, and the heat, and the piles of uncollected rubbish made the streets intolerable. Our only link with the outside world was our transistor radio. I would switch from station to station, listening as each claimed its love for Lebanon and its promise to defend it, crying shame on the other political parties. The only news we trusted were the broadcasts from Monte Carlo and the BBC World Service. Armed men were everywhere, even youngsters carrying guns, and you constantly ran the risk of being attacked in your own home, kidnapped, or simply evicted. One woman told me how she pleaded with those who had invaded and occupied her house, asking them if they would allow her just to retrieve a few personal belongings. 'No,' was the answer. 'Go away. You own nothing.'

I would stand on one of our balconies in the evening and see all the neighbouring houses which had been abandoned by their owners. Smoke was rising from a bombed-out office block. Down in the street, people were hurrying home, afraid. Cats rummaged through the rubbish heaps. I could hear shooting. From the AUH, I could hear women screaming and sobbing in voices which cut through the night, mourning their dead. I will never forget the sight of one woman. It was most probably the body of her son laid in the funeral car and her family were trying to persuade her to get into another car. She was screaming, standing in the middle of the street and beating her chest, her face grimacing hysterically, rejecting her son's death by not moving from the hospital gates where she felt there might still be hope. Eventually, three men pushed her into the car. They drove off, accompanied by loudspeakers chanting the well-known Koranic verses: 'Do not consider those who died in the cause of God dead, but living with God.' I was haunted by the woman's sorrow, her shattering grief, and asked myself whether anything was worth such suffering.

Because of the danger, we had to replace our ordinary wooden doors with iron ones and put lockable gates in the entrances to the flats. Attempts to visit parishioners became perilous – we had to tell people in advance, usually on the preceding Sunday, that we would *inshallah* (God willing) visit them on such a day. They would wait for us by the window or on a balcony, and come down to open the main gate, or let down a key in a basket for us to open the gate and then climb the stairs. You dared not risk using the lifts, for fear of a power cut which would leave you imprisoned.

I would look at my mother, sitting on the sofa with her eye-glasses and her aluminium walking-stalk, and feel filled with love and pity for her. So old and frail, yet still peaceful in the midst of such troubles. 'Mama, are you all right?' 'Yes.' 'Mama, do you want a cup of tea?' 'Yes, please.' Tea-time to my mother was like a sacred ritual. Her disabilities were a continuing source of concern and sorrow for me. She had lost the sight in her right eye because of glaucoma and had suffered a detached retina in the other, but to our relief it had been operated on successfully. I was never a good sleeper and as her health deteriorated, I would wake many times in the night, at the slightest sound, and go to her room to make sure she was safe and well.

In the nine years we lived in Beirut, not a day or night passed without shooting. The dead and wounded were brought to the AUH, with members of the different factions shooting in the air to force other cars and passengers out of the way, as well as to honour the dead. Many, many times bullets found their way to our balconies. Some of our acquaintances and friends were kidnapped. I remember in particular the Revd Benjamin Weir, a gentle pastor who had worked for years in Beirut and spoke Arabic fluently. He was taken by Islamic Jihad as he walked from his house, and held for four months. And yet Beirut was an extraordinary city. Buying and selling went on. Demonstrations and festivities went hand-in-hand. Beautifully dressed women would skirt the rubbish heaps in their high heels, on their way to the jewellers, the florists, the boutiques. The street vendors outside the hospital would stand aside to let the funeral cars pass, and then go back to selling their heaps of fresh oranges, apples, plums, crisp green vegetables.

Church Life

Before the war, the Anglican congregation had worshipped in a beautiful church in a prestigious setting on St George's beach, near a number of expensive hotels. It had been built and maintained by the expatriate community for the Beirut chaplaincy which was created in 1887. In 1976 it was hit in one of the battles, 'The Battle of the Hotels', which raged over the control of the port of Beirut, each side determined to crush the other, whatever the price. On one of the few occasions when we dared to drive in that area, we found it frightening, a ghost city pocked with gunshots, filled with deserted shops and restaurants, broken walls and roofs. Shadowy figures of slum-dwellers and armed youngsters emerged from the ruins to watch us.

Our congregation worshipped in the chapel of the newly-built School of Theology, a bare place with a big glass window overlooking the street. The grey cement walls were ugly, and if you looked up to the roof, perhaps in the hope of spiritual uplift, you saw only a thick brown pipe running across it. The only relief for the eyes came from the beautiful flower arrangements put on the altar by one of our parishioners. In time, we gradually improved the place, changing it into a simple, decent place of worship. What was still gratifying, though, was the human church, the living stones. They were lovely people, resourceful, practical, steadfast, quick to co-operate. Rafiq introduced coffee after church, and this proved a great time for coming together and drawing strength from the fellowship, especially for those who were confined to their homes for long days and nights because of the shooting in the streets.

Jameeleh was the name of a woman who helped me with the housework in our Beirut home. She came from northern Syria, from a district called *Wadi e-Nasara* (Valley of the Christians), and was a good worker, always willing to do what was needed. She told me how she had been engaged to a man and noticed that he liked her sister. She asked her sister if she liked him. When her sister said yes, Jameeleh's reply was, 'No problem. You take him.' She used to look after the family cows at home, but her sister-in-law wanted her out of the house and beat her so much that she eventually left with her sister and came to Beirut. Every month she would buy food, clothes, cassettes of the latest Arabic songs, and travel to her home village along dangerous roads, first to Tripoli and then crossing to Syria. It would take her seven hours, sometimes much longer, to get to the village where she gave the presents to her unwelcoming sister-in-law who would send her back with a new list of requests. She would cry as she told me the latest episode in this sad drama.

We would talk about Beirut, sharing its tragedy, crying as we watched the funeral processions leaving the university hospital. We would work in the house together, airing the rugs, cleaning the windows, washing the floor, dusting the ornaments, ironing the covers, leaving all fresh, clean, shining at the end of the day. Such days were special, though. There was not always enough water for such work, even though Rafiq had installed an extra water tank so that we could save more when the taps were operating. It became commonplace to see professors, doctors, housewives, people used to living in comfort and even luxury, queuing in the street for water with plastic buckets and bottles, and then climbing the many stairs back to their flats, because the lifts were out of order.

Our Family's Travels

Our daughter Karma was studying at Bir Zeit University when we moved to Beirut, and she preferred to stay there at least for her first year. By the end of that year, however, she had decided to join us, because the situation in Bir Zeit was not easy owing to Israel's continuing policies of harassment and closure. Later she decided to study English Literature at the American University of Beirut (AUB). This University was founded by Protestant missionaries in 1866. My late uncle and many members of my family, as well as my husband and my daughters, studied there. It kept its doors open with American aid and philanthropy and had a beautiful campus sloping down to the Mediterranean, with fine buildings, pine and cedar trees, tennis courts and gymnasium, even its own beach. Life at the AUB was not what a young student might have imagined, however. Fear and disruption haunted the lives of both parents and students. Sometimes the professor would not turn up. Outside there was constant sniping and shooting. Some days there would be a strike or a day of mourning – or fighting. On one day a battle was raging outside the hospital and in the street outside our house. Youngsters with anti-tank weapons were at the gate to our apartments, while the doctors were trapped in the hospital. A good day at AUB simply meant being able to attend a lecture and come home safely.

Our daughter Randa was by now in the United States studying anthropology. In one of her rare letters she said she was coming back. We were thrilled, and waited to hear more. Months passed and she did not come. We wrote to her address but received no answer. We wrote to her friends. Nobody knew anything. One day, at mid-morning, there was a knock at the door. I was serving coffee to a church friend and opened the little spy-hole to see who was outside. I glimpsed a young girl and took her for an AUB student – some of them would come round, from time to time, to ask questions for their research – but the girl said, 'Come on, open the door.' In a flash of realization, I knew it was Randa. I do not know how I opened the door, but I remember grabbing hold of her and dancing round the room. Our friend stood watching with tears in his eyes and on more than one occasion afterwards, he told me that he would never forget that scene. Soon Randa was to tell us that although she had come home, she intended to lead her life the way she wanted. This meant a whole-hearted dedication to the Palestinian cause. 'Only a greater love for the people will save the people,' she would say. She threw herself into the life of the refugee camps, working alongside volunteers from abroad – Americans, Europeans, Palestinians born overseas.

When Nabil finished his education in Swansea, he came to Beirut and found a job as a civil engineer with Dar el-Handasa, an architectural firm with projects all over the world. We enjoyed having Nabil living with us but I was always worried about him because he would go out with his friends in the evening and sometimes not return until very late. I would lay awake at night or wait out on the balcony, fearing the worst as I heard bombs exploding somewhere. I was relieved when he eventually got a job in Abu Dhabi.

Amin was living in Jeddah with his family. It was wonderful when they visited us for the first time in Beirut for Christmas. Amin did not like what he saw of Beirut and once said to me, 'Are you surprised that there is war in Lebanon?' I thought he was talking about the sectarianism. 'No,' he replied. 'The class divisions, the very, very rich and the deprived.' I had never seen it that way before, but he had a point. Lebanon had been the playground of the international rich, while so many lived in utter poverty in the same country.

Another welcome visitor came as a complete surprise. I went to answer the door-bell and saw a woman standing there. As I cautiously looked out at her, she said, 'Open the door. I am 'Irfan's wife.' My brother's wife! Excitedly, I pulled the door open and embraced Mary, hardly believing that at long last I was meeting her in the flesh. I rushed her to my mother's room where she was lying in bed, broke the news, and then brought Mary in. My mother wiped away the tears she could not restrain, and tried to take in the fact that Mary was her daughter-in-law. Mary said that she had come to Beirut to visit her family and that 'Irfan was lecturing in the Gulf countries and would be coming in two days' time. It felt like the sun coming out from behind dark clouds, and my mother and I basked in the warmth of it, in the joy of meeting my brother and his wife.

17
Death in Beirut

Early in 1979, I received a letter from the Jerusalem YWCA, inviting me to represent the Middle East at a conference in Athens. The theme was 'The role of the YWCA in a pluralistic society'. I accepted gladly, little knowing the trouble ahead. For many years now I had been suffering from an irregular heartbeat. In Ramallah I had been put on medication but the problem had never been taken seriously, because it had always stabilized in the end. The night before I was due to leave for Athens, however, my heartbeat began racing so fast that I could not count it, then slowing right down, even stopping for a moment. In the early hours of the morning, Rafiq took me to the hospital outpatients where I was given an injection. It had no effect and so I was taken to see the heart specialist and rushed to intensive care. The monitor showed the sharp ups and downs, the symptoms of an irregular, troubled heart. For seven days I lay in the intensive care room, learning that what I suffered from was called 'atrial fibrillation'. It meant that the electricity of my heart went wrong. I was put on new medication for life and have continued to suffer from the condition to this day. I was very disappointed to miss the conference, but my speech was sent on and was read by one of the other delegates.

One day I had a phone call from Mrs Agaby, one of our church members. 'I have been trying to get a call through for quite a while. Please come this afternoon to meet a visitor of ours who is bringing a woman guest from America. This American woman would like to speak to us.' 'No, I can't.' 'Please come. I can't manage by myself.' 'Manage what?' 'You know, one needs to be able to quote texts because such speakers have a rhetoric all of their own. We must be able to present our point of view.' 'I'll try my best.' 'No, I want you to come.' Reluctantly I went. Nobody else turned up, so the meeting consisted of me, Mrs Agaby, the Arab visitor and her

American friend. The American woman was well groomed, with a confident manner, and began leafing through a much used Bible. She read out prophecies and other extracts from the Old Testament, building up an argument to prove God's faithfulness to his chosen people up to the present day. There was no mention of Jesus or his message.

When she had finished, I pointed out that the focal point of our belief was Jesus and the cross, and that he had given a new interpretation to the ideas of the promised land and the chosen people. She did not like what I said and seemed nervous. Then we heard shooting outside. Soon after, Mrs Agaby's husband Emile came in, his face very pale. 'There is a battle in Hamra Street,' he said. 'I found myself in the thick of it.' 'I must get home,' I said, sensing the danger. 'You can't. There are armed men everywhere. One of the militia leaders has been killed.' I decided to call Rafiq, but the phone was not working. 'Stay,' pleaded Mr Agaby. 'There is no reason why you should leave.' 'No, I must go back.' It was getting late. I had a terrifying walk. I was the only person out and the sound of my footsteps on the pavement was very loud. I kept noticing armed men with angry faces standing in doorways. At one point two men stopped me but then allowed me to continue. The last hundred metres or so were the most frightening. My home seemed to recede as I walked, heart pounding. Perhaps I would die on the doorstep. Never had a short distance seemed so far. I rang the bell. Nobody answered so I let myself in. Rafiq must have gone out to find me. Time passed very slowly until he returned, having driven through side-alleys back from the Agabys' house where he had gone only to discover that I had left already. It was good that we were both safe.

Next day there was a sizable presence of Syrian National Party militia in the streets. As one of the opposing sides in the Hamra Street battle, they had come out to honour the dead. As the coffins emerged from the hospital, uniformed men and women saluted and marched off to accompany the procession.

Tragically, Mr Agaby disappeared in 1983 as he travelled back to Beirut along the road from Shtūra near the Syrian–Lebanese border with a young student. Neither of them were ever seen again and they were eventually presumed dead. In another tragic episode, a young student, Waleed Jamil

Shehadeh, returned from studying in the States, left the house during a lull in the shooting, and never returned home. His family eventually traced his mutilated body via a newspaper photograph.

Graduation Day

At last the day came for Karma's graduation from university. Even in such a troubled situation, parents and relatives came from far and wide – Jordan, the West Bank, Syria – for such a great occasion. As was customary, the university President held a garden party on the night before the ceremony for students and their parents. I remember how happy and relaxed I felt that evening, enjoying the pretty garden, the cool breeze, the throng of beautifully dressed students, the friends and relatives visiting from abroad. The sky was illuminated by thousands of twinkling stars. We could hear shooting not far away but it seemed to have nothing to do with this crowd of people on such a happy occasion. I felt no need to hurry home as Randa had stayed to look after *Teita* (grandmother). When we arrived back at our apartment, I went into the kitchen, set down my bag, put on my apron and started whisking cream for cakes specially made for Karma's graduation party. For some reason, I did not go to see my mother first. Then Rafiq and Randa appeared at my side. In a strange voice, Rafiq said, '*Teita* is no longer with us.' I turned and saw their faces and rushed to my mother's room. She had slipped away in her sleep, while Randa had been in the other room.

Rafiq rang the doctor, my immediate family, and my brother in the United States. Under the circumstances, it was felt best that her body should go to the hospital. Even death in Beirut was full of hazards – where should the funeral take place, when the church graveyard was out of bounds to us? My brother could not come because the airport was closed and travel was too dangerous. I resigned myself to not attending Karma's graduation, even though I had not had the privilege of being there for any of my other children. On the following morning, however, we discussed the matter with friends and they persuaded me that I should go, for Karma's sake and in memory of my mother. So, one day before the funeral, I sat among the crowd, watching the procession of the graduates, listening to the speech by Ihsan 'Abbas, Professor of Arabic Literature, but mostly looking at the old, dark cypress trees that stood on the hill above the stadium where we were sitting.

The sun's rays shone fiery red through the branches and for a moment, as I thought of my mother's living and dying, I felt as if past, present, and future came together in a mysterious way. I watched Karma come forward to receive her certificate, shake hands with the President, have her photo taken. Then the day was done, a symbol of civilization in the middle of warring, miserable Beirut.

Next day we held a short service for my mother in the university chapel and then moved on to the Baptist church. Rafiq and my daughters sat beside me. We sang 'Abide With Me' and a couple more of my mother's favourite hymns. I thought of her playing the organ. I thought how much I loved her. I cried. She was buried in the cemetery at Ras e-Nab'aa. Few people came, because it was dangerous. We laid flowers on the grave which was not far from the resting-place of one of my cousins. For the next three days, as was the custom, people came to give their condolences. I had never realized how much my mother was loved by all who had known her. Even as I write this, the tears come back, wetting my glasses, obscuring my vision – but ever since her death she has somehow remained a presence in my life.

Karma went on to study for her MA, while working in the Family Bookshop in Hamra, one of a chain of bookshops linked to the Middle East Council of Churches. Sometimes the surrounding area was exposed to gunfire and I was terrified, expecting the worst. When Karma reappeared at the front door, I felt as if she had come back from the dead.

A Visit to North America

Rafiq's parents and many members of his family had emigrated to Canada and a few to America. In 1980, Rafiq felt it was time he should visit his parents who were by then getting on in years. To get a visa in Beirut for North America required lots of stamina and endurance. The queue was long, even if you arrived very early. The area where you had to queue was, like everywhere else, not safe from shells and bombs. Sometimes the embassy would close, when you were nearly at the door, waiting to be interviewed.

Meeting my in-laws in Toronto was a strange experience. I remembered Rafiq's parents in their old house in the village of Shefamr, surrounded by a garden filled with trees – orange, grapefruit, olive and pomegranate. Rafiq's father would climb the pomegranate tree, even at the age of eighty, and pick the best fruit for us, bringing it with him when he next visited us in Ramallah. At the end of their years, he and his wife had faced the choice of staying in their homeland or venturing abroad in the steps of their children who had already moved to Canada. I was happy to see how well they were and how the welfare state offered so much for people of their age.

I loved Canada, its trees, the newness of the countryside, the vastness of the horizons. It felt like a country in the making with its mixture of people, all equal as citizens of Canada. On later visits – such as our 1983 trip to the World Council of Churches conference in Vancouver – I learnt more about the inevitable social problems and the pain that is often part of a large immigrant community. Later we visited New York, where another Palestinian relative of Rafiq's, Canon Sameer Habiby, ran the Refugees Department at the Episcopal Church Centre, under the auspices of what was called the Presiding Bishop's Fund for World Relief. When he heard that Rafiq had come from Beirut, he arranged for us to speak at a number of events, giving first-hand accounts of events in the Middle East. Not far from the Episcopal Centre I could see the United Nations headquarters, housed in its glass palace, and I thought of the peoples of the Third World who saw the UN as their last resort, the place to plead their causes, believing in justice and human rights.

Staying with some friends we had first met in Beirut, the Blackstones, we found that arrangements had been made for us to be photographed and interviewed by the press about the Middle East. Next day more than one local paper carried the story under the headline 'Palestinian Couple Take Plea to Christians', telling how a Palestinian clergyman and his author wife were conducting a 'soft-sell campaign' in the US to gain recognition for their people. Reading the article, I thought how weak I was, how small our voices, how helpless our people. Again and again we faced the same questions – what about the

Holocaust? The Bible? Terrorism? Little Israel surrounded by Arab countries? Nasser? It was so hard for the rich and powerful countries to hear, to want to hear, what we were saying.

Sunday 24 August 1980. St Andrew's Episcopal Church, Oklahoma. Rafiq preached on the theme of 'We Stand Together':

> More than 40,000 Lebanese have been killed in the last four years and about 200,000 people became homeless. The story behind all this tragedy and continued suffering goes back to 1948. One of the reasons was that the West felt guilty because of what Hitler did to the Jews, and created the State of Israel. From 1948 till this day, however, Israel has had no peace. All its economy is geared to more and more military preparation and more and more sophisticated weapons.
>
> But from 1948 the Palestinian people were thrown out of their homes and lands and prevented by Israel from returning. They experienced and are still experiencing great suffering. Two million Palestinians became refugees and are still dreaming of their homes and lands. They are not terrorists but real people and all they want is to go back to their country. They are entitled to the basic human rights of home and land, and the right to determine their political future.
>
> My wife and I are speaking to Christians in the churches. We are not coming on a political crusade. We are speaking to you as Christians, for all this is affecting the Church in the Middle East.

Rafiq went on to speak of the threat posed to the indigenous church communities by immigration, of church buildings lying empty, of a land without a living Christian witness. He thanked Christians in the West for economic aid and relief but stressed that this did not solve the problem, the injustice. The Christian churches had to put pressure on their governments to bring about a peaceful solution which involved the right of three million Palestinians to determine their own future.

Invasion

In the summer of 1982 Israel launched its invasion of Lebanon, with the name of 'Peace for Galilee'. The very word 'peace' made me shudder, reminding me of hearing the word used by Ben Gurion in 1948, when it was always followed by some dreadful attack on towns and villages. It took Israeli troops only a few days to reach Beirut, sweeping across the countryside, destroying refugee camps such as 'Ein el-Hilweh near Sidon, the home of 24,000 refugees, killing over 10,000 people, most of them civilians. I remember the massive aerial bombardment of Beirut and South Lebanon beginning on 4–5 June – I noted the dates, remembering 4 and 5 June 1967, in Beit Hanina on the West Bank. I cannot describe those days of bombardment. They were shapeless, unreal, millions of bombs pouring on to West Beirut like a gigantic, devilish concert staged in the air, at sea and on land. The whole city shook, smothering fires blackened the buildings with soot and swirls of smoke. I remember one Saturday when 24,000 bombs dropped from the air, aircraft swooping down like vultures and leaving trails of blood and flesh, innocent blood and flesh.

Rafiq and I hid in the corner of our bedroom, not able even to talk to each other. Randa, her baby Bashar, and Karma were with us. Randa became very afraid for her baby. Whenever she heard the aircraft coming, she would rush to me, the baby in her arms, her face pale. 'Mama, they've come.' 'It's all right. Stay with me.' Karma was calmer, more resigned.

The deadliest and most destructive American weapons were dropped on Beirut indiscriminately: cluster bombs, phosphorus bombs and suction bombs fell on refugee camps, residential quarters, apartment buildings, schools, air raid shelters, hospitals and embassies. At this time, when Rafiq took funerals for those who had died of natural causes, people consoled the bereaved. 'Thank God that he died a natural death. Alas for them that died burnt or flayed or under the rubble.' I remember a writer visiting our house with a friend who had just received news that his brother and all the family had been killed in an attack on one of the refugee camps. I said how sorry I was and, trying to say something more, asked, 'When is the funeral?' His friend looked at me reproachfully, saying only, 'No funeral. They are all dumped in one hole, with all the others who died.' I had no words to give an answer and eventually went to the kitchen to make coffee and hide my tears.

On 11 June Israel declared a cease-fire against the Syrians who were not keen to continue their war on land and in the air – but there was no cease-fire with the PLO. Israel turned on the Palestinians who were surrounded in West Beirut, dropping leaflets which urged the inhabitants to leave the city and save their own lives. Two hundred thousand out of 500,000 left Beirut, but those who stayed continued the fight with great courage and skill. Along with the terror-bombing, the Israeli army laid siege to Beirut for two and a half months. Life became very grim as water, food, electricity and petrol became scarce. Contrary to all human rights laws, they did not even allow through supplies of milk, blood or medical equipment for the hospitals. We heard that milk was poured out at the roadblocks rather than be allowed to enter the city.

On 2 July the PLO stated its decision to withdraw but the siege and bombing did not stop. The stench of death in the streets increased. At home, we tried to be brave, to act normally. We even renewed the tradition of tea-time. When the shop on the ground floor of our block was open, we bought a small sort of fruit cake known as English cake, and spread a white tablecloth with a lace border, rang a little brass bell and announced afternoon tea to the family. Later that month, we decided that Randa, Karma and little Bashar should go to Beit Miri in the mountains, to a school where we thought they might be safe, despite the dangerous journey. When they arrived, however, they realized their situation was in fact more dangerous because they were Palestinians in an area dominated by the Phalange (a paramilitary organization founded by the late Pierre Jamai'el, a Maronite political leader, in the middle of the thirties), where the Israeli occupiers were actually welcomed by the local people. They were advised not to speak to anybody outside the centre, in case their accents were detected. Very soon they were desperate to come back to Beirut and before long, they were able to make the return journey.

It was not until 19 August, after weeks of that terrible bombardment, that a satisfactory agreement was reached between Israel and the PLO, the main worry of the Palestinians being the fate of the families in the camps if the men left. The agreement was that the US would guarantee the safety of the Palestinian refugee camps while Israel undertook not to enter West Beirut. What in fact happened will be forever remembered as the Sabra and Shatila massacres of 16–18 September 1982, when the Israelis permitted Lebanese militiamen to go into the camps on a slaughtering rampage. They killed men, women, children, even horses, dogs and cats. We were in England at the time and watched public concern growing at the horrific TV pictures and newspaper reports of the events.

Writing – how do you write in such a situation? Some might think that in such tragic circumstances there is ample material to use, but I did not find that to be the case. The events choked me, the enormity of the collective suicide that is civil war. I felt that whatever I wrote would only scratch the surface and would involve taking sides, but sometimes I caught a moment when I sensed I had encountered truth of some kind, and that stirred me to put pen to paper.

I was involved in a Beirut committee for children's book-publishing and even attended a conference on writing for children which took place in Cyprus. The plane journey took maybe twenty minutes from Beirut, yet I felt a cloud lifting from me on that island of beautiful beaches and olive trees, where women sat over their needlework in peaceful villages, and flowers bloomed outside the houses. One of my books was reissued in Beirut under a scheme to reprint books relating to Palestinian Mandate times or even earlier. Alas, at that very time the Palestinians were about to leave Beirut and in the event many of these projects were either destroyed or came to a standstill. I never knew what happened to the 3,000 copies of my book. Three of my novellas, under the title of *A Journey of Grief and Giving*, were published by the publishing house Dar el-Kalemeh. I received three or four copies, but then the publisher's offices were bombed and burned to the ground. Thousands of different books were lost, including mine, and the publishers were forced to close.

In 1985 I took a trip with Rafiq to the diocese of Melbourne, Australia, at the invitation of the Archbishop of Victoria, David Penman. When we had lived in Haifa, Rafiq had sometimes mentioned Australia as somewhere he could possibly emigrate, but the idea had always been impossible for me. What would I do in such a faraway country when the breezes among the olive trees of Palestine rushed to my memory? But when we actually arrived, I saw how easy it could be to switch your mind from the old world. Of course Australia has many problems – as does any country – but I found a meeting of East and West which somehow created something quite new. In the gardens and parks, the trees brought from the West stand side by side with the gum trees and bush shrubs. There is nostalgia for the old country, for the past, but also a defiant sense of new life, of separate identity.

Many Arabs had moved to Australia and in Sydney there is a whole part of the city where a Lebanese dialect of Arabic is spoken. We met a former headmaster of St George's School in Jerusalem there and I was astonished to find how settled he and his family were, so far away from what had been home. I began to wonder whether I too could find a home, a new home, in another part of the world, but I know that the breezes among the olive trees will always be the source of my joy and tragedy.

I must say that Archbishop Penman was a great supporter to the Palestinians. He died a few years ago. A clinic was opened in his memory in Zababdeh, a Palestinian village near Nablus in the West Bank.

18
Remembering Palestine

15 June 1986.

To all our friends: God willing, we shall be in London after the second week of July 1986. We are invited to do three things there: to help in a Church of England parish two days a week; to carry out a pastoral ministry to Arab Anglicans and other Arab Christians; to be available for consultations on the Middle East. We leave Beirut in a much worse situation than when we arrived in January 1977 . . . there is a polarization and fragmentation of society, with chaos and anarchy rooted in daily life . . . gun fights in the streets are a daily occurrence . . . almost all Westerners have left Beirut, for fear of being kidnapped . . . the West and East of Beirut are still divided, and exchange of sniping and shelling has continued between the two sections of the city almost daily for the last eleven years. In spite of all this we hope and pray for peace . . .

People thought I would be relieved to leave Beirut, but I was not. Something inside me was pulling me to stay. I came to realize that in grief and sadness there is an intensity of involvement which normal life does not create. Lebanon was a country which I had always loved and I had desired to end my days in a little village somewhere in its beautiful, peaceful mountains.

Instead I found myself in a taxi, cautiously manoeuvring a way down the familiar streets, through the chaotic drivers on the main road by seashore, to the airport. I looked at the tall palm trees, the glistening waters of the Mediterranean. The crumpled houses and mangled cars by the roadside looked like relics from ancient times, resigned to their fate. Goodbye, Beirut. Goodbye, Middle East. Goodbye, forty years of work, of ministry. How short a time it seemed, no more than a dream.

After spending time with Karma at her new home in Cyprus, we flew to Heathrow Airport where Amin met us and drove us down the M4 to his home in Wales. Even in his beautiful garden, welcomed by his wife Carole and their children, I felt lost, sad, unsettled by the unbroken quiet after years of hearing bombs and shooting. Since that arrival in 1986, we have made a home for ourselves in Britain. Both Rafiq and I have had many opportunities both in the UK and abroad to speak about the Christian presence in the Holy Land and the Palestinian situation, and we have enjoyed ministering to Arab Christians in the UK, holding services in our own language. A highlight of recent years has been meeting Barbara Butler, wife of the Bishop of Leicester and founder of 'Christians Aware', an ecumenical and cultural movement with the main aim of developing understanding and friendship between different groups of Christians locally, nationally and internationally. Together with Barbara and another talented friend, Joan Biles, I worked on two publications: *Palestinian Pain and Promise* (an anthology of poetry, stories and essays) and *The Colour of Courage* (a selection of my writing). I have also enjoyed the friendship of Alistair Duncan of The World of Islam Festival Trust, an organization concerned with Christian–Muslim understanding. It is partly through this support that this book has come into being.

I also began writing for an Arabic women's magazine, circulated mainly in North Africa. As well as printing my stories and novellas, the magazine put me in charge of their problem page. Most of the letters were about unrequited love, sent by young men and women struggling with relationships in situations weighed down by cultural tradition and patriarchal authority. I always advised them to speak out and not depend on others to solve their problems. Another highlight has been the founding of 'Living Stones', an ecumenical group whose aim is to send Christian individuals and groups from the UK to the Holy Land, to meet the Arab Christians there, listen to their story and seek to understand their problems. Since the beginning, Rafiq has been a member of the group's committee.

When I think of the struggles of the Palestinian people, I think that perhaps it is not the heroic deeds that kept us going, but the patience, determination and resilience of the Palestinian women. They kept house, cooked dinner, washed the clothes, looked after the babies, proving that family life, love and care, home duties and school, could go on even in a refugee camp. There are many educated women who have contributed to the Palestinian cause, but above all there are the illiterate, dispossessed women who maintain the identity of our people, identifying themselves and their families by the name of the villages, the orange groves, the olive trees, left behind years before, their embroidery preserving the traditional patterns of their communities.

In 1988 I went to Sweden to address the Women's Association of the Church of Sweden Mission. Part of my trip included a visit to Umea, 400 kilometres from the Arctic Circle, a place of seemingly endless snow. At a meeting there, I met to my surprise a Palestinian woman in a headscarf, her five young daughters with her. She had heard that a fellow countrywoman was coming and had been waiting impatiently to see me. I could not hold back my tears. The woman was in her forties, her daughters were teenagers, dark-haired, smiling, eager. 'Where are you from?' I asked the girls. 'Acre,' came the reply. 'But we were born and brought up in 'Ain el Hilweh (one of the Lebanese refugee camps). Our mother moved from Acre as a very small child.' What could these girls know of Acre? I wondered. Oh, they knew everything, the great walls, the history. Yes, they would one day go to Acre. They did not belong in the long twilight of that snow-bound city, but were rooted in the orange groves of the Palestinian coast and the walls of Acre, where little boys jump into the blue waters of the Mediterranean. 'Where is your father?' I asked. 'He is imprisoned in Ansaar.' Ansaar was a place which became one of the most gruesome of Israeli prisons after the Israeli invasion. The mother told how he was tortured, forced to put his hand flat on the floor by a door which was then opened and shut, tearing off his fingernails. He was released once, when the family was given permission to come to Sweden. He insisted that his wife and children use the travel papers and go ahead of him, but he never followed. His wife suspected that he was in prison again.

Although everybody was kind to her, and she had been given a flat, and the girls were studying, she missed the refugee camp, her friends, their home community. Now they were so far from home, in winter twilight, the Baltic Sea freezing white on the beach and the lights of Leningrad shining over the water.

Our children, settled round the world, thrive with their families. Even though we no longer live in the Middle East, we have followed events closely – the *Intifada* (the Arabic name for the Palestinian uprising in the West Bank and Gaza Strip that broke out on 8 December 1987, a grass-roots movement spanning all age groups and social strata), a sign of hope for so many Palestinians worldwide, the Gulf War, and then the Peace Settlement, yet the memories of the Palestine I once knew stay with me. The winds of Jerusalem, swaying the trees, Christmas celebrations at the YMCA, the hills of Nazareth turning dark violet as evening approaches. In the night I hear the sound of the wind, exciting and mysterious. Where does it come from? Where is it going? I long to journey with it. The stars shine, twinkling yet elusive – and I remember, sharp as a pain in the heart, the starlight through the fig trees and olive trees of my homeland.

Suggestions for Further Reading

Farah, Najwa K., *The Colour of Courage*. Christians Aware, 1991.
Fisk, Robert, *Pity the Nation*. Oxford University Press, 1992.
Khalidi, Walid, *Before their Diaspora*. Institute for Palestine Studies, 1991.
Mansfield, Peter, *The Arabs*. Penguin, 1992.